# The Greatest Trades of All Time

Founded in 1807, John Wiley & Sons is the oldest independent publishing company in the United States. With offices in North America, Europe, Australia, and Asia, Wiley is globally committed to developing and marketing print and electronic products and services for our customers' professional and personal knowledge and understanding.

The Wiley Trading series features books by traders who have survived the market's ever changing temperament and have prospered—some by reinventing systems, others by getting back to basics. Whether a novice trader, professional, or somewhere in-between, these books will provide the advice and strategies needed to prosper today and well into the future.

For a list of available titles, visit our Web site at www.WileyFinance.com.

# The Greatest Trades of All Time

## Top Traders Making Big Profits from the Crash of 1929 to Today

VINCENT W. VENEZIANI

**WILEY**

John Wiley & Sons, Inc.

Published by John Wiley & Sons, Inc., Hoboken, New Jersey.
Published simultaneously in Canada.

For general information on our other products and services or for technical support, please contact our Customer Care Department within the United States at (800) 762-2974, outside the United States at (317) 572-3993, or fax (317) 572-4002.

Wiley also publishes its books in a variety of electronic formats. Some content that appears in print may not be available in electronic books. For more information about Wiley products, visit our web site at www.wiley.com.

*Library of Congress Cataloging-in-Publication Data:*

Veneziani, Vincent W., 1986–
    The greatest trades of all time : top traders making big profits from the Crash of 1929 to today / Vincent W. Veneziani.
        p. cm. – (Wiley trading; 483)
    Includes bibliographical references and index.
    ISBN 978-0-470-64599-4 (cloth); ISBN 978-1-118-13462-7 (ebk);
    ISBN 978-1-118-13463-4 (ebk); ISBN 978-1-118-13464-1 (ebk)
    1. Speculation–History.   2. Stocks–History.   3. Investors–History.   4. Business cycles–History.   I. Title.
    HG6041.V46   2011
    332.63'2280973–dc23

                                                                                          2011017549

Printed in the United States of America

10   9   8   7   6   5   4   3   2   1

*For Grandmère. I love you.*

*It is not by augmenting the capital of the country, but by rendering a greater part of that capital active and productive than would otherwise be so, that the most judicious operations of banking can increase the industry of the country.*

—Adam Smith

# Contents

# Acknowledgments

There are so many people to thank in the process of writing this book that all of them can't be listed here. Writing a book is a challenging process. It requires extensive research and time commitments like no other task. So to all of you who stood by me while I wrote, I thank you.

First and foremost, I'd like to thank everyone at John Wiley & Sons for making this possible and for offering me the opportunity to write a book on a topic that I truly love. My editors, Kevin Commins, Meg Freeborn, Jennifer MacDonald, and Melissa Lopez were a huge help through the entire process, and I simply couldn't have finished this book without their support and guidance.

Next, I'd like to thank everyone in the financial community who gave me their opinions or helped me understand things I needed help with. To Kyle Bass and Jim Chanos: Thank you for taking time out of your days to let me interview you on your trades.

I would like to extend a special thanks to William Yeack, David Rucker, and Adam Jastrzebski at Golden Archer Investments. William proved to be an invaluable asset in helping me unravel the intricacies of the global financial markets from an insider's viewpoint. Based on the trajectory of his career, this young hedge fund manager will surely be included in a later edition of this book!

Louis Yeung, Evan McDaniel, Laz Hansen, John Carney, Allan Schoenberg, Jon Najarian, Andrew Coffey, Mick Malisic, Jordan Terry, and the StockTwits team (Jeremy, Phil, Justin, Leigh, and Howard) have all played a special part in one way or another in helping me write this book. A special thanks goes out to Mohan Virdee, David Griffiths, Terry Flanagan, and the rest of the team at Markets Media—respecting the industry that puts money in our wallets and food on our table is very important to me.

Finally, I have to thank my friends for their overwhelming support. Neil Ruben, Ben Burton, Steve Weitzman, Ryan Ash, John Biggs, Nick Deleon,

Julia McCloy, Courtney Comstock, Stephanie Ochal, Darlene Dobkowski, Antonina Wiktoria Jedrzejczak, and anyone else who I may have missed.

A special thanks to Kimberly Schroeder for putting up with me during the editing process—I know it wasn't easy for you. You have been wonderful and I will always have a special place in my heart for you. And also for Stella, be it cat, ficus or anything else.

And of course, my family has been more supportive than anyone else. Thank you, Mom, Dad, Alice, Sean, and Ryan, Grandmère, Bill and Bell, Kate, Conner, and Joseph! I love you all.

# About the Author

V incent William Veneziani is a trader and writer on markets, financial news, hedge funds, and economics for financial publisher Markets Media. He has also appeared on CNBC, Russia Today, and the BBC as a commentator.

Previously, Vincent worked at Business Insider covering Wall Street and the economy. He has also written for Gawker Media, AOL, *New York Daily News*, *Popular Mechanics*, and TechCrunch.

Vincent currently resides in New York City.

# Introduction

I n the past 100 years, financial innovation has quite possibly reached the apex of its evolution. Debt instruments, investment services, and changes to market structure have changed, for better or for worse, and we the people have changed with them.

There is a certain breed of man that is unmatched in terms of genius and business acumen. These "demigods" of the financial world have played such an important role in economic development in modern times that their absence would dramatically alter the life-changing events such as the financial crisis of 2008–2009.

Within every market lies opportunity. Whether you are long or short does not matter, but how you play the game does. People like John Paulson and Kyle Bass identified profitable opportunities when they were but a brief idea in the heads of their counterparts at major banks and other institutions.

Through discovering these various opportunities, these men and these men alone executed what I consider the greatest trades of all time. It must be noted that I am not being sexist by any means. The fact is that no woman and very few men have achieved what the people in this book have.

One must not forget that the game is played in a multitude of forms, whether it is fixed-income markets, derivatives, equities, or some other financial instrument. They are all interconnected. Economies of the world are interconnected as well and thus trying to remove worries like systemic risk from our world will be impossible during our lifetime.

The ultimate goal of this book is to engage and educate the reader. For the longest time, I never took an interest in finance. When I executed my very first trade to see what the fuss was all about, I was immediately hooked. I read every book, every web site, every white paper. I needed to know not just how certain things like the stock market worked, but how *everything* worked. Finance is my life, and I'm sure it is the same for the people mentioned in this book.

Facts are also important. I have done as much as I have to ensure that everything in this book is factual. I have also gone through great lengths to help readers understand how some of the more complex transactions work.

In the past few years, the Wall Street culture has been vilified by those not involved in it, such as political groups and the media. I hope that this book will help to educate some on what really goes on in the minds of giants and their financial institutions.

While the rage over pay associated with billion-dollar trades is understandable, realize that without the economies that currently exist, as well as the banks, the players, the traders, and everyone else, the world would be a far different place. One of my favorite examples is the futures markets. They started as a way for America's farmers to hedge against price fluctuations in commodity markets and still serve that purpose, though the futures markets have evolved quite a bit since then.

I am sure that some readers will not agree with the ways that these men achieved their unprecedented wealth and fame, but remember this: Across the world, economies create and destroy wealth every day. The spirit of the free market combined with stunning entrepreneurship and economic prowess is just one component that makes the world go 'round.

I truly hope you enjoy reading this book as much as I enjoyed writing it.

VINCENT WILLIAM VENEZIANI
New York
*August 2011*

# The Greatest Trades of All Time

## CHAPTER 1

# J. Kyle Bass

*Timing Is Everything*

O ut of all the legendary men in this book, perhaps the least known is J. Kyle Bass. A hedge fund manager from Dallas, Texas, Kyle is a young, energetic and brilliant man who is not exactly of the Harvard Business School pedigree. Educated at Texas Christian University, the elusive Bass is one to be reckoned with. He is famous for shorting the subprime mortgage crisis that enveloped our country late in the first decade of the 2000s.

But don't be fooled. The man is as shrewd as hedge funders come. Bass saw the crisis coming back in early 2006, when the stock market was peaking and everything was still fine and dandy. Only 36 years old at the time, Bass was one of the youngest managers in the business to spot the crisis coming and to actually place a large bet on it.

## THE BACK STORY

Bass started his career as a retail securities broker at Prudential Securities before moving on to Bear Stearns & Co., Inc. and later to Legg Mason, Inc., where he stayed until January 1, 2006. While Bass had plenty of success working for Wall Street firms, in December 2005 he decided it was time to strike out on his own.

Starting your own hedge fund is a daunting task that requires intense preparation. And then there is the capital—who is going to give you capital if no one's heard of you? You are just another face in the crowd.

Bass, not just any regular face in the crowd, was able to raise an adequate amount of money for his new fund, Hayman Capital. The fund would be sufficient, but not overburdened, and Bass got to work researching investments.

It is extremely important to be familiar with the tale of derivatives and subprime, second-lien mortgages that unfolded after Bass set up Hayman Capital, and, to truly understand and appreciate the financial alchemy that is in Bass's story, you need to be well educated. First and foremost in the story of Kyle Bass are subprime mortgages.

## A FEW DEFINITIONS

Most people understand what a mortgage is, but what about a subprime mortgage? An easy way to think of it is to break down the word *subprime*. What do you think of when the word *prime* comes to mind? For some, it's steak. So you've got a prime cut of steak, like a filet mignon, or perhaps a not-so-good cut that is *under prime* quality. Devalue it further in the case of subprime, and you get the drift; *sub*, of course, means "under" in Latin. Thus, one takeaway is that a *subprime* mortgage is a mortgage that leaves much to be desired for an investor. And that raises the question, "If you're an astute investor, why not just toss out the crappy mortgages and buy up the good ones?" The answer is easy: the process of turning something into a security known as securitization. Stocks, bonds, and Treasuries are all securities, so why not securitize mortgages? It even makes sense on paper. Mortgages provide a steady flow of monthly payments to the originating lender or bank that can then be used to service debt.

A mortgage-backed security (MBS) is created when a firm (usually an investment bank) packages a pool of mortgages together and creates debt instruments that are backed by the cashflows and collateral of the underlying mortgages. For years it was viewed as a fool-proof investment because it seemed like everybody would win. Mortgage originators would sell a group of mortgages to a securitization firm (usually an investment bank) or, in the case of larger financial institutions that originated mortgages, they would handle the securitization process themselves. This process allowed originators to clear the loan portfolios off their balance sheets and free up capacity to originate more loans and make more fees. A genius idea, really. But why stop there when having a stroke of genius?

Initially, people securitized mostly prime mortgages. As the demand for MBS increased, the market soon realized it could securitize and sell lower-credit quality mortgages. It accomplished this by offering multiple classes of debt backed by the loans. The classes or "tranches" would vary in interest rate and payment terms, with more senior tranches generally being repaid first and as a result yielding a lower interest rate. To best explain the idea of tranches, think of an Olympic medal ceremony. There are three winners (who we'll compare to the investors in our mortgage scenario), and they are delineated into gold, silver, and bronze medalists. The gold medalist is at the top of the podium and a safe bet due to his consistent performance. The gold medalist represents the top tranche, and as you could imagine, it doesn't provide a staggering rate of return. The top tranche is the first to receive cash from the mortgage pool (and importantly the last to absorb losses). In our example, an investor may get close to a 4 percent return by investing in the top (gold) tranche—little return for little risk.

Then there is the silver medalist, who may have had a few bad runs in the course of an Olympic career, but generally is a decent and respectable contestant to put a wager on. The silver medalist is like the second tranche of MBSs. They have a little more risk, but also a little more return for the risk. The second tranche will return close to, say, 6 percent. This tranche is slightly more risky because it will experience losses from the mortgage pool before the gold does.

And finally, we have the bronze medalist. Bronze is the bottom tier. While few people bet on bronze, if bronze pulls out a win the payout would be significant. The bronze medalist represents the riskiest portion of the securitization because its tranche is the first to absorb any losses from the underlying mortgages and the last to be repaid from the cashflows. However, if a sufficient number of homeowners pay off their mortgage or do not default until the later stages of the payments, the bronze tranche would be repaid. In this example, the bronze tranche would earn 8 percent because of the additional risk.

In summary, the first tranche is nearly risk-free and thus has a very small rate of return. The second tranche is a little more risky but pays out a little more than the first. And bronze is the riskiest tranche of them all but, should it work out, pays out very nicely.

## BASS ASKS WHY

With that brief MBS 101 lesson behind us, we head back to 2006, when J. Kyle Bass started Hayman Capital. At the time, home ownership in the United States was near an all-time high and home prices were continuing to climb. Bass noticed, however, that average income in the United States was not keeping pace. He sat there wondering how exactly this was happening. If home prices were climbing but average income was not increasing at the same rate, how were home buyers able to obtain mortgages to purchase homes and continue to drive prices up? He decided to investigate the mortgage originators (the lenders) who were getting people with no credit or bad credit—and in some cases no jobs—into homes.

A lot of politicians in the United States have always pushed the belief that home ownership is a good thing and that everyone should have access to the ability to own a home. It's part of the American dream, for sure. But it doesn't always work out that way or, at least, it shouldn't. Should a 20-year-old making $2,470 a month with three jobs be allowed to get a $183,000 mortgage backed by the Federal Housing Administration with just 3.5 percent down? History has already been the judge on this one, and the answer is a resounding "no." For those of you without a house, 3.5 percent of a $183,000 mortgage equates to about $6500—a ridiculously small amount for a down payment.

And this is just one example, mind you. In simple terms, all over America, predatory lenders were out searching for people sign up for mortgages—in some cases by any means necessary—so they could collect the *fee*s while passing on the actual *risk* to a bank or investment firm. In addition, once secured, the mortgages would then be sold to securitization firms that had little incentive to scrutinize the original borrowers. So, what started out as a genius idea turned out to be a no-holds-barred game of deceit because of a number of complicated factors.

And what deceit it was! Some lenders would approve potential homeowners with just a name, Social Security number, and any kind of identification. A typical conversation could be imagined to have gone along these lines:

**Lender:**     "All right, Mr. Johnson, so we're going to give you a $250,000 adjustable-rate 30-year mortgage. How's that sound to you?"

**Borrower:**   "Fantastic! I've always wanted to live in my own home and stop renting. But there is a problem..."

| | |
|---|---|
| **Lender:** | "And what's that?" |
| **Borrower:** | "Well, I don't have a job right now and I also have six credit cards. Oh, and I work two jobs and have a car loan that's outstanding, too." |
| **Lender:** | "No problem! Let's just make it up as we go along. Sound good to you? I really want to get you into this house. Think about how much easier your life will be when you're a homeowner!" |
| **Borrower:** | "Yeah! Okay. Sure! Let's do it!" |
| **Lender:** | "Great! I'm going to take 20 minutes and go grab some lunch. When I get back I want to see some details on a job, your annual income, and your list of debts on this paper, if you get my drift." |

Sounds unimaginable, right? But if you think I'm being a bit too absurd, think again. As part of his investment research, Bass hired private detectives, who uncovered interactions similar to the conversation just described. In an interview I conducted in March 2010, Bass told me that the loan originators he found in 2005 and 2006 were the absolute lowest of the low. They, and the organizations they worked for, preyed upon the public interest in home ownership and tried to exonerate themselves from the ethical challenges of such work by employing the underbelly of the earth: drug dealers, convicted felons, and any other similar type of creature that came along. Not just the "regular Joes" but the "really bad guys."

For a number of reasons, almost no one could see this web of lies, money, and mortgages destroying the country one loan at a time, but one of the few exceptions was Kyle Bass. He simply looked at the data from his research and said to himself: "Something doesn't make sense here." Of course, this behavior was atypical at the time, but Bass is a man with a voice and mind-set different from the status quo. He once convinced JP Morgan to help him finance a portion of his house in Japanese yen on the bet that it would ultimately be cheaper than the U.S. dollar.

Kyle Bass has always made the case that companies, no matter how big or small, should be subject to the concept of fiscal Darwinism: The weak perish while the strong survive. Should American International Group, better known as AIG, have been allowed to fail and the taxpayer spared billions? In his mind, the answer was "absolutely."

Politicians were oblivious to what was going on. Anyone with a basic understanding of economic theory knows that a country cannot continue to print money as it wishes while racking up gigantic deficits. Throughout the period of subprime lending, home prices continued to soar to new highs as Americans' incomes failed to keep pace. Without both factors working together, the spread between the two became wider and more dangerous. And that is exactly what Bass saw happening when he took a deeper look into the activity in the market. He recognized that this country was giving everyone and their uncle an opportunity to own a home despite the fact that home ownership was well beyond their means. Maybe it was proof that, as Jeff Kreisler said in his book *Get Rich Cheating*, "The American dream is just that: a dream."

## LEARNING FROM THE PAST

Undoubtedly, the worst part of the financial crisis of the late 2000s is the fact that we actually had an opportunity to learn from our past mistakes. In 1998, the year when John Meriwether was blowing up his hedge fund, Long-Term Capital Management, another crisis was unfolding. Bass described this in great detail during our interview:

> *I don't know if you remember, but back in 1998, there was a sub-crisis. 1998 was a time in which there were companies that were high loan-to-value (LTV) second-lien lenders.*
>
> *Okay, so what these guys would do was, they would make these high LTV loans like 125 percent at loan-to-value loans and they would be second liens. So think about your priority in that position: You're never going to collect if anything ever goes wrong. So they were hiring PhDs and trying to figure out what the incidents of default on these second-liens were going to be. And the bottom line was, again, there were convicted felons making these mortgage loans. And at the time, there were many Wall Street firms that just didn't care, packaging these things up and securitizing them. This is back in '98, so '96, '97, '98 second liens. So that market blew up in 1998.*
>
> *All those companies went bankrupt except for...one which was acquired by another firm. And it almost brought down the other firm. It eventually was spun out in bankruptcy to a private equity firm.*

Think of 1998 as a test run for the housing crisis of the late 2000s. Adding further fuel to the fire, a lot of the people who ran these firms went and started subprime mortgage origination shops in 1999 and 2000! It was a time when subprime mortgages were the last thing on regulators' minds.

The American people hadn't even heard the term because in 1999 and 2000, the tech boom and dot-com IPO era was making millionaires overnight at an astounding rate. America was in good times and letting the good times roll.

In addition, the people running these firms were not just middle-level managers with their own greedy agendas. They were also CEOs, CFOs, and principal partners who all ran the companies right into the ground and then started right back up again in another venue. It was a vicious cycle.

Shady lending will continue to be the de facto way of lending to the nation's poor and less fortunate until a proper set of regulations and conditions are put into place. The fact that convicted felons have the ability to offer someone a home loan and approve or deny it seems unethical at the least. And the corruption does not stop there. In the early 2000s, if you thought a homebuilder has built too many homes, you were essentially laughed off. Money flowed freely, thanks to the Federal Reserve, and as a result, private-equity deals were happening left and right. If you bet against a homebuilder by going short, the next day you'd discover the firm had gone private and was now safe from your speculation. It was all rigged: Enron, home prices, the U.S. monetary system, and of course, the façade of regulation. In 2006 and 2007, Bass geared up to make one of the biggest bets of all time: shorting the subprime housing market.

## SHORTING SUBPRIME LOANS

To *go short* is to bet that prices will fall and, in terms of the housing market, fall they did. In late 2006, as new home loans began to seize up and credit tightened, prices inflated. Through the use of derivatives, Bass and his newly created Subprime Credit Strategies Fund reaped the benefits of this crisis by investing in derivatives that enabled them to profit if the housing market tanked.

Bass explained in detail how he couldn't wait to launch his fund:

> *I literally couldn't wait one more day. I was so afraid that this [situation] was going to crack before I got the money raised. And remittance data comes out on the 25th day of every month and I couldn't wait for one more bit of data to come out. So I was fearful that we had spent all this time doing work, in-depth research, and modeling mortgages and, when I was meeting with investors, I'd say, 'We need to raise this right now.'*

If you saw it coming, you'd want to prepare yourself to go short immediately, too. Bass elaborated:

> *In July of 2006, you had, on average, about two million homes in inventory for the last five or six years in available-for-sale inventory. And what you saw was that inventory, by the end of '06, had moved up in six months' time to four million homes. So what you saw was prices leveling out, you saw inventory massively building, and then you saw at the very end of 2006, the whole loan pricing starting to come down. So we launched [the Subprime Credit Strategies Fund] in the middle of September of 2006.*

It should be made clear that derivatives are not evil. They are not the devil incarnate unleashed into the hands of greedy young traders. Derivatives are a perfectly legitimate tool for hedging and protecting yourself from bets made in markets. After all, the word *derivatives* is just a fancy way of saying that an instrument or contract derives its value from the value of some other instrument or contract. Futures are a type of derivative. A farmer may sell a futures contract to smooth his cash flow and lock in a certain value for his crop. Is that so wrong? Similarly, a bank may use derivatives to hedge against its outstanding loans in case they default or get a ratings downgrade and lose part or all of their value.

Now that you can appreciate the value of derivatives, no matter your opinion, you can see that Bass speculated that the housing market was about to crumble.

## THE BEST POSITION

In February 2007, Bass began to orchestrate one of the greatest trades of all time. We already know Bass had researched his investment thesis and uncovered the shadier practices of certain mortgage originators. These originators secured customers for the banks and were paid handsomely in fees for performing the mundane task. It didn't matter that the customers could afford only the first few years of interest-only payments on a home loan. As long as the originator booked it and got the fee, the repercussions of what could (and in this case, what did) happen later were moot.

Bass reminded us that mortgages are more than just numbers for accountants and actuaries to crunch. They also contain a qualitative aspect:

> *What you had to figure out was there's the quantitative aspect of things and there's the qualitative aspect of things. And the quantitative aspect, everybody had. Everybody had [all the] terabytes of mortgage data, modeling software that they could buy.*
>
> *But the qualitative aspect was kind of: who were the originators that had literally no standards at all?... So what we did was, we went out and we found the bad guys.*

Bass found plenty of bad guys. He investigated the lifestyles and backgrounds of these mortgage originators and their companies. Who were they? What was their incentive to offer someone making $30,000 a year a $500,000 loan? Clearly something was amiss, and Bass was able to exploit the small window of opportunity where the economy and housing market began to turn just a tad sour. Originally, he claims, he wanted to find out if the originators were "fine, upstanding members of the community just trying to earn a buck" or whether they were "guys that had big drug problems that were financing themselves and their crazy lifestyles with mortgage origination."

If you think about it, the point Bass makes is scary. Twenty years ago, when credit wasn't flowing like a broken faucet in the United States, someone looking for a loan would have to go to the bank and speak with a man in a suit and show the proper backup in order to justify the loan. It was a trusted process, and there was plenty of due diligence on both sides of the transaction. Flash forward to 2006, and there you are telling an ex-convict how much you want a loan and you have no way to back it up. Salary, debt-to-income ratios, and other important factors of a loan were simply tossed out the proverbial window and made up on the spot in order to satisfy the banks. These loan originators collected their fee and then repeated the process with more and more customers until satisfied with their income.

Bass saw hints of the coming mess as early as 1998. Looking back, it seems like the warning signs were everywhere and becoming more frequent, popping up every week practically as 2007 neared. In that year, toxic loans were still being made, but not at the pace of previous months and years. By the time the market and the U.S. government began to realize that something was up, it was too late; Bass had already gone short and was entering a position that would ultimately become one of the best of his life.

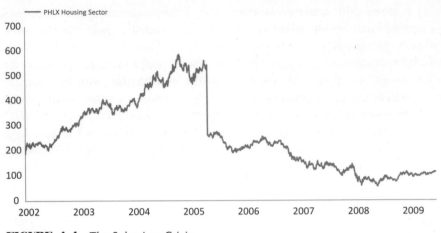

**FIGURE 1.1**  The Subprime Crisis
*Data source:* Historical data from Yahoo! Finance

The housing crisis is ultimately a complicated web that's hard to un-tangle but Figure 1.1 shows just how complex the system really was.

As Bass's investors began to see profits, like anyone making a decent rate of return, some investors became inclined to redeem and book their profits up to that point. Bass says during that time, he insisted that in-vestors leave their money in the fund so it could truly grow. His point: If you double your money, that's fantastic. But what if you could earn a lot more on the investment? That's what Bass really had in mind. Investors would inquire about redeeming and Bass would retort, "Are you kidding me?" The move he was making was an opportunity of unprecedented scale. In the months leading up to the crisis, an investor could throw a dart at a stock and watch it go up with the rest of the stock market as the Dow hit new highs and continued to climb without care. But when things turned sour with housing and credit, it was Bass's investors who began making the big bucks.

In February 2007, the Subprime Credit Strategies Fund was kicking into high gear. By July 2007, the fund was up over 100 percent. That's 100 percent return on investment in six months! Any investor would be smiling ear-to-ear if after hearing that within such a short period their investments had doubled. One million dollars turned into $2 million, $10 million into $20 million, $100 million into $200 million. And Hayman Capital was one of the hottest (albeit relatively unknown) hedge funds on the block.

It should be made clear that the counterparties to the investments made by Bass were large securities dealers, not homeowners who were losing their houses. Bass's investments were in derivatives that got their value from the default rates of the lower-rated mortgage securitization tranches. The American people and investors of the world suffered due to the lack of governmental oversight of the mortgage industry at many fundamental levels. A jaw-dropping example of this is found in a book by Henry Paulson, a former Goldman Sachs CEO and former secretary of the Treasury, *On the Brink: Inside the Race to Stop the Collapse of the Global Financial System*. It is a tale of how even our own secretary of the Treasury did not have a clue about what was going on until it was too late.

Indeed, quite scary.

## THE EFFECTS OF ABUSE

The housing crisis turned into the credit crisis, which turned into the financial crisis. In a little under four years, home values plummeted like a rock off a cliff. One could argue, though, that it was simply the market correcting itself after years of abuse. While this may be true, it doesn't negate the fact that millions of Americans lost the shirts off their backs and got stuck in homes with mortgages costing way more than they were worth. In many cases, these were people who had reasonable credit histories and had been making their mortgage payments each month—they weren't even a part of that risky third tranche.

Because of this domino effect, job by job, bank by bank, loan by loan, things began to crumble. First Bear Stearns stood on the brink of collapse; it was ultimately bailed out for $10 a share by JP Morgan. Then came the highly leveraged Lehman Brothers and Merrill Lynch, which were sold off to Barclays and Bank of America, respectively. Countrywide. AIG. General Motors. When would it stop? The United States and its financial industry came to a screeching halt.

In 2006, Bass started shorting subprime housing lenders and subprime mortgage insurance providers, and he shorted them hard. And just as his gamble began to really pay off, our nation saw economic collapse of unprecedented proportions. Ten percent unemployment may not sound like a large number, but when you realize that means that almost 1 in 10 Americans is without a job, it is humbling. To get an idea of how unemployment looked up until 2008, see Figure 1.2.

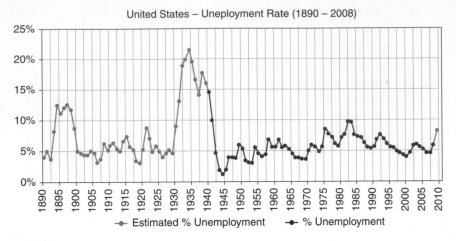

**FIGURE 1.2**   Unemployment Rate

Most of those out of work will file for unemployment benefits, and this contributes to rising governmental costs and adds strain to our national deficit. Add that stress to the burden of the home the unemployed have been paying on for 10 years with an adjustable-rate mortgage, which will soon balloon to a payment they cannot afford (never mind the foreshadowed mortgage payment increase; they are unable to make the current mortgage payments) and expand it by millions of people, and you start to see the magnitude of the situation. The bank that lent the homeowner the money will foreclose on the house, contributing to its balance sheet losses. And even worse, the housing market has collapsed, and the house is now worth substantially less than its purchase price. The restaurant down the street where the homebuyer ate twice a week is now seeing him twice a month, and it continues to lose money. The restaurant cannot afford to pay all its employees, so it lays off a few of them. The vicious cycle repeats itself in additional venues until divine intervention by either God or the Federal Reserve arrives.

To underscore the impact of the recent financial crisis, see Table 1.1, which presents data from the St. Louis Federal Reserve.

At the start of 2005, unemployment was at a respectable 5.3 percent. In 2006 it fell to 4.6 percent, where it stayed until 2008, when the crisis really kicked into high gear. It then shot up to where it stands at the writing of this book: 9.7 percent, which is a little lower than the 10.1 percent unemployment rate of October 2009. Will the economy improve? Perhaps. The last time we had double-digit unemployment was in 1983.

**TABLE 1.1** St. Louis Federal Reserve Data, 2005–2010

| Year | Month | Unemployment Rate |
|------|-------|-------------------|
| 2005 | January | 5.3% |
| 2005 | June | 5.0% |
| 2006 | January | 4.7% |
| 2006 | June | 4.6% |
| 2007 | January | 4.6% |
| 2007 | June | 4.6% |
| 2008 | January | 5.0% |
| 2008 | June | 5.5% |
| 2009 | January | 7.7% |
| 2009 | June | 9.5% |
| 2010 | January | 9.7% |

If you take a cue from Bass and stress the importance of numbers, you can look at any presentation of mortgage data for the past decade and the number of loans in delinquency or default and correlate the data with Table 1.1. You will notice the pattern of worsening home sales and rising unemployment. The same can be said for retail sales, consumer confidence, and many other economic measures.

## WHO WAS WATCHING?

Where were the governmental regulators when we needed them most? Well, aside from dealing with Enron and WorldCom in the early 2000s, regulators were relatively inept in their ability to spot the potential crisis. After all, the only reason that companies like Enron and Lehman Brothers were in the news is that a dreadful lack of regulation had failed to catch the misdeeds of these companies. And when it's too late and the shareholders have been wiped out, that's when it becomes important to the Securities and Exchange Commission (SEC) and Financial Industry Regulatory Authority (FINRA). It happened about the same time as people started to see the scandals on the five o'clock news.

Kyle Bass went around talking to people throughout the financial community in 2010 in an attempt to explain just how serious the situation had become. He posed an incredible question: "What business do you know that is a trillion-dollar business that directly touches a consumer that's unregulated? Save for mortgage origination, there isn't one." He drove home the point that could have very well prevented the previous three years of recession, poverty, and job loss:

> *We need to regulate mortgage origination. Period. At both the bank and non-bank, at state and federal [levels]. I don't care where the regulation is but it needs to be firm. Right? They need to set firm debt-to-total-income ratios, just coverage ratios saying, "This is what you can do and you can't do anything else." It just makes sense.*

During our interview, Bass became more intense and showed a true passion for wanting to stop the nonsense in the housing market. For sure, he could wait for another crisis to come along, go short, make more money, and be on his way. But I believe that's not how Bass sees himself overall. Yes, an extraordinary opportunity brought him a boatload of money, but unlike other investors, Bass would like to also see a change come out of it: an end to the predatory lending of the past decade and a clear direction on where this country is headed in terms of regulation and finance.

One issue for Bass is that even if regulators imposed strict lending standards and prevented people who can't afford a home from getting into homes, a sizable portion of the United States' population would suddenly find themselves segregated. It is why we have Freddie Mac and Fannie Mae, why the Federal Reserve keeps a close watch on the economy, and why the Federal Housing Authority exists. Bass explained that if we simply did away with all the bureaucracy and put in place set-in-stone laws and regulation, it would cut out a sizable portion of existing mortgages and future lending prospects. This type of restriction would cause major consequences. In a more regulated market, banks couldn't lend to as many people and couldn't take in as much money as they'd like. Thus, non-home loans from banks would begin to become scarce. Fannie and Freddie would have no way of buying home loans because there simply wouldn't be enough to guarantee. Asset-backed securities tied to home loans would shrivel up, soon followed by auto loan-backed securities, credit card-backed securities, and so on, up until there was simply a minimal amount of credit flowing. The securitization business would soon grind to a halt. This is all, of course, somewhat of a worst-case scenario, but we need to keep it in the back of our minds. Remember: Everything in an economy is ultimately systemic.

Further, our government is part of the problem, not a solution, and it is a matter of fiscal responsibility, not politics. Taking a cold, hard look at government-sponsored entities Fannie Mae and

Freddie Mac, Bass discussed how we're just postponing a long overdue problem with these bailed out GSEs:

> *Well, you look at Fannie and Freddie, right? [The U.S. government has] already given them $181 billion, and it is not in the Obama budget by the way, and if you look at the 2010 budget or the 2009 budget, that $180 billion is in never-never land. It's not in the budget. Fannie and Freddie are going to cost taxpayers over $400 billion when it's all said and done.*

Think about what Bass is saying: $400 billion. The savings and loan crisis at the end of the 1980s cost the taxpayers $120 billion. We've given $181 billion to Fannie and Freddie alone. Even if you adjust for today's dollars, our GDP was half of what it was back in, say, 1988. So even if you double that number to $240 billion, just Fannie and Freddie alone are going to lose $400 billion. And we've already written down about $900 billion for the banks. It's almost incomprehensible. But people seem impervious to it. They say, "Oh yeah, what's a billion trillion dollars? It doesn't matter. I don't even know what numbers that large mean." But it's very relevant especially when thinking in terms of size. And the Fed's answer has been to keep printing money. Ben Bernanke, later chairman of the Federal Reserve, said in 2006, "I wouldn't worry, I have a printing press!" And he's using it.

Hank Paulson, former Goldman Sachs CEO and secretary of the Treasury under President George W. Bush, agrees. In his book, *On the Brink*, Paulson details how he believed a sweeping overhaul of Fannie and Freddie were needed in order to prevent them from imploding under their own weight. Paulson tried to get Congress to see the problem, but it ultimately was a lost cause. It was also a shame, considering that the foresight of Paulson and others like Bass had could have prevented our deficit from taking on another couple of hundred billion dollars from bailouts. And really, the deficit is the key. Figure 1.3 showcases the U.S. deficit as a percentage of GDP from 1970 through 2010.

After 2005, when the financial system began to collapse, the cost of these bailouts skyrocketed the deficit to unprecedented levels. It was double or triple that of some years past. It is funny to think that as little as 10 years ago our deficit was a surplus.

Now that our debts have climbed above 10 percent of our GDP, printing more money will only delay the inevitable. At the time of this writing, Fannie and Freddie equity was trading at around $1.10 and $1.35 a share, respectively. These are penny stocks that would no doubt be delisted from

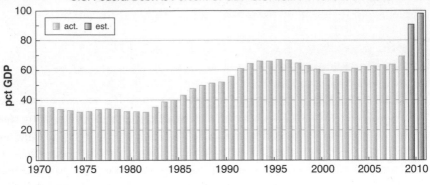

**FIGURE 1.3** U.S. Debt

an exchange if it weren't for their government bailout and conservatorship. Bass spoke in our interview of how this situation mirrors that of United Airlines in 2002:

> *Nobody knows where Fannie and Freddie will be 5 to 10 years down the line. I don't know. You've got to handicap the politics of Fannie and Freddie because the financial aspects of Fannie and Freddie should be in receivership. It's now in conservatorship, which is never-never land—it's the Twilight Zone. And still, it's theoretically public that the taxpayers are losing up to $400 billion and there's still public equity that trades, which should be wiped out.*
>
> *Think about this: United Airlines was in bankruptcy for a number of years. There was a point where they were about to emerge from bankruptcy and then the equity was wiped out and the subordinated debt was only worth 18 cents. Essentially, the stock was worthless, but it was trading hundreds of millions of shares and it went from $1 to $3 because the general public was watching CNBC and heard United was about to emerge from bankruptcy. The public then bought the prebankrupt, preconditioned equity and lost all their money. It just goes to show you that people have no idea what they're doing.*

It is when people do not understand what they are doing that other people profit from it most. As the housing market, government-sponsored enterprises, and economy all took a turn for the worse in late 2006, people like Kyle Bass made the most of the situation and profited handsomely. While some may decry the practice of a fund turning a healthy profit in a time when the macroeconomic picture of things is headed downward, one must remember that there is always a way to turn tragedy into money.

## RE-CREATING BASS'S TRADING STRATEGIES

The thing about Kyle Bass that makes his trade difficult to replicate by the retail investor is one big concern: capital. Bass had plenty of capital and is an accredited investor who is capable of buying complex instruments. But the main themes we can learn from behind his trade involved two things: the housing crisis and mortgage originators.

A way you could short the housing market involves futures contracts based on specific real estate markets offered by CME Group. These contracts are based on the Case-Shiller Home Price Index, the de facto standard for a gauge of America's housing situation.

Table 1.2 shows contracts offered by CME Group. For instance, say you thought Chicago's housing market was going to be in shambles between now and May 2011. You could sell the May 2011 Chicago S&P/Case-Shiller Home Price Index contract and hope that the underlying index for that contact falls in value. You would then buy it back at a lower price and profit.

If you're not acclimated to futures trading or you don't have the capital for that sort of trade, another way to play the housing market would be to short homebuilders. This can be done via an exchange-traded fund (ETF) offered by State Street Global Advisors (the Homebuilders SPDR ETF), trading under the ticker XHB. Simply short the ETF and, should the price drop, buy it back and profit.

In Figure 1.4, you can see the five-year performance of XHB. Clearly, this ETF took a huge hit during the recent financial/housing crisis.

While this may not reap you the sort of returns that Kyle Bass and his investors saw, it's a solid, easy way to play the same sort of trade.

## BASS'S TOP TRAITS

Kyle Bass is one of the greats. Few people saw the subprime housing crisis coming from so far, and he performed his fiduciary duty to his clients to the fullest effect, netting them returns in triple digits. The housing market may very well never return to the levels seen in the past unless we experience an

**TABLE 1.2** Real Estate Calendar

| Comm Code | Exch | Month Code | Contract Name | Product Type | Last Trade Date | Settle Date |
|---|---|---|---|---|---|---|
| BOSG11 | CME | 201102 | February 2011 Boston S&P/Case-Shiller Home Price Index | FUT | 02/18/2011 | 02/22/2011 |
| BOSK11 | CME | 201105 | May 2011 Boston S&P/Case-Shiller Home Price Index | FUT | 05/27/2011 | 05/31/2011 |
| CHIG11 | CME | 201102 | February 2011 Chicago S&P/Case-Shiller Home Price Index | FUT | 02/18/2011 | 02/22/2011 |
| CHIK11 | CME | 201105 | May 2011 Chicago S&P/Case-Shiller Home Price Index | FUT | 05/27/2011 | 05/31/2011 |
| DENG11 | CME | 201102 | February 2011 Denver S&P/Case-Shiller Home Price Index | FUT | 02/18/2011 | 02/22/2011 |
| DENK11 | CME | 201105 | May 2011 Denver S&P/Case-Shiller Home Price Index | FUT | 05/27/2011 | 05/31/2011 |
| CUSG11 | CME | 201102 | February 2011 Housing Composite Index | FUT | 02/18/2011 | 02/22/2011 |
| CUSK11 | CME | 201105 | May 2011 Housing Composite Index | FUT | 05/27/2011 | 05/31/2011 |
| LAVG11 | CME | 201102 | February 2011 Las Vegas S&P/Case-Shiller Home Price Index | FUT | 02/18/2011 | 02/22/2011 |
| LAVK11 | CME | 201105 | May 2011 Las Vegas S&P/Case-Shiller Home Price Index | FUT | 05/27/2011 | 05/31/2011 |
| LAXG11 | CME | 201102 | February 2011 Los Angeles S&P/Case-Shiller Home Price Index | FUT | 02/18/2011 | 02/22/2011 |
| LAXK11 | CME | 201105 | May 2011 Los Angeles S&P/Case-Shiller Home Price Index | FUT | 05/27/2011 | 05/31/2011 |
| MIAG11 | CME | 201102 | February 2011 Miami S&P/Case-Shiller Home Price Index | FUT | 02/18/2011 | 02/22/2011 |
| MIAK11 | CME | 201105 | May 2011 Miami S&P/Case-Shiller Home Price Index | FUT | 05/27/2011 | 05/31/2011 |
| NYMG11 | CME | 201102 | February 2011 New York Commuter S&P/Case-Shiller Home Price Index | FUT | 02/18/2011 | 02/22/2011 |
| NYMK11 | CME | 201105 | May 2011 New York Commuter S&P/Case-Shiller Home Price Index | FUT | 05/27/2011 | 05/31/2011 |
| SDGG11 | CME | 201102 | February 2011 San Diego S&P/Case-Shiller Home Price Index | FUT | 02/18/2011 | 02/22/2011 |
| SDGK11 | CME | 201105 | May 2011 San Diego S&P/Case-Shiller Home Price Index | FUT | 05/27/2011 | 05/31/2011 |
| SFRG11 | CME | 201102 | February 2011 San Francisco S&P/Case-Shiller Home Price Index | FUT | 02/18/2011 | 02/22/2011 |
| SFRK11 | CME | 201105 | May 2011 San Francisco S&P/Case-Shiller Home Price Index | FUT | 05/27/2011 | 05/31/2011 |
| WDCG11 | CME | 201102 | February 2011 Washington D.C. S&P/Case-Shiller Home Price Index | FUT | 02/18/2011 | 02/22/2011 |
| WDCK11 | CME | 201105 | May 2011 Washington D.C. S&P/Case-Shiller Home Price Index | FUT | 05/27/2011 | 05/31/2011 |

*Data source:* CME Group, www.cmegroup.com

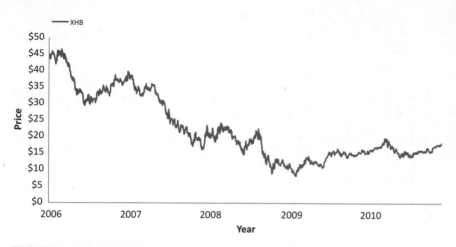

**FIGURE 1.4** XHB Chart
*Data source:* Historical data from Yahoo! Finance

inflationary economic period of accelerated proportions. If that happens, you can bet Bass will be going over the charts again.

Bass's trading style exemplifies talent that is rare. Here are a couple of reasons why he profited so magnificently from his greatest trade:

1. Foresight: Kyle Bass is a thinker. When the numbers don't add up, he really thinks about the situation and constantly asks why. He also has history on his side. Bass is incredibly knowledgeable on everything related to economics, finance, and everything in between. He predicted the housing crisis because he didn't like what he saw going on with mortgage originators and related issues after doing research.

2. Persistence: Bass wouldn't budge when investors came knocking at his door. When the going got tough, he knew he was right and didn't move. He stayed cool and assured everyone that they would make money if they held on a little longer.

■ ■ ■

Bass will undoubtedly become one of the most successful investors ever due to his clear thinking during the unique time that was the 2000s, and it will be interesting to see what his next big payoff is. Again, players like Bass are few and far between. When they become known for their trades, pay close attention and listen to what those trades are saying.

In the next chapter, you will learn about one of the best short sellers.

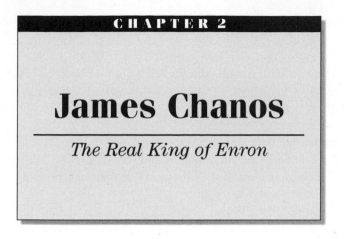

## CHAPTER 2

# James Chanos

## *The Real King of Enron*

J im Chanos loves Girl Scout Cookies. Thin Mints, to be exact. He struts into the conference room of his hedge fund, Kynikos Associates, with a box of them in tow. He sits down and offers me one before we begin our long talk about how one man became a billionaire off Enron while Enron burned to the ground. It plays out a bit like the fall of Rome, except with higher stakes.

Chanos, a Yale-educated short seller, is without a doubt the most famous trader in this book. He started his fund, Kynikos Associates, in 1985 with an adequate amount of capital, an amount that easily made it so he could short distressed firms to his heart's content. And no company would be safe. From Drexel Burnham Lambert to Tyco to Boston Market, Chanos shorted them all and took with him a princely reward. His talent was for spotting companies that were bound for failure.

## ENTER ENRON

Enron came to prominence in the 1990s. Because of its demise, Chanos would ultimately end up making the greatest trade of his life. Shorting Enron was incredibly lucrative due to the longtime extent of corruption within the company. The company would go on to become the largest bankruptcy the United States has ever witnessed, and Chanos was along for the entire ride.

Before examining the trades associated with the collapse of Enron, we must first examine what exactly Enron was. Enron Corporation was an energy company. However, it was not an energy company in the sense that Enron was delivering heating oil to your grandmother in the winter. Enron was an energy services company that did everything from buying and selling energy to trading energy and broadband Internet, among other things. The company was so complex and its ventures so intertwined that it is easy to become confused as to what the company actually offered to the public. But let's give it a shot.

Back in the 1930s, Enron began as a company called Northern Natural Gas Company. Northern Natural Gas Company bears little to no resemblance to the modern Enron, of course. In 1979, NNGC became a subsidy of a holding company called InterNorth, which went on to acquire the Houston Natural Gas company in 1985. The iteration of the company as Houston Natural Gas would help lay the groundwork for the modern Enron. Half a year later after its 1985 acquisition, InterNorth spun off the Houston Natural Gas subsidiary into what would technically become known as Enron Corporation. It was at this time, after InterNorth purchased Houston Natural Gas, that Enron CEO Kenneth Lay arrived in the mix.

Lay was a free market advocate who was highly intelligent and had close ties to the Bush family. In the movie *Enron: The Smartest Guys in the Room*, Lay's wife (now widow) describes how she used to call Lay "Kenny Boy" on frequent occasion. President George W. Bush soon adopted the same nickname for his friend, Ken, demonstrating the familiar relationship between the two parties. Lay helped Enron become one of the largest energy companies in the United States over the next two decades. The company grew rapidly from the late 1980s into the early 2000s as it laid pipe and electricity lines and did other large infrastructure deals that solidified its position as a dominant player in the energy market.

During that time, Enron made acquiring companies one if its top priorities and spent a lot of dollars marketing itself as God's gift to the energy world. Internal initiatives like these bolstered Enron's stock price, which eventually hit a high of $90 in August 2000. The high stock price in turn made many Enron executives (as well as employees) very rich. As we know, money has great power to corrupt. And, in Enron's case, that is exactly what it did.

## *REALLY* LOOKING AT ENRON

Jim Chanos began to observe Enron from a distance in the early 1990s and noticed how it was a rapid acquirer of companies. One of the questions he asked himself was, why acquire rather than innovate in-house? He realized it was because Enron didn't need to innovate in order to grow. Enron was involved in everything from futures trading of sugar and plastics to online trading of energy. It was involved with so many kinds of businesses, it is truly staggering. The following lists demonstrate just a few of the areas it was engaged in. Enron traded:

- All manner of products on EnronOnline (its commodity trading platform) including:
  - Petrochemicals
  - Plastics
  - Power
  - Pulp and paper
  - Steel
  - Weather risk management products
- Broadband products
- Principal investments
- Commodity risk management products
- Products from the shipping and freight industries
- Water and wastewater products
- Oil and liquefied transportation products
- Streaming media products

They were also involved extensively in futures. At the time of its bankruptcy filing in December 2001, Enron was structured into seven distinct business units, each with its own large and complex web of sub-departments/businesses. You can see a large listing of some of the pieces of these businesses, and start your own research into how far-reaching Enron's dealings went, if you visit Wikipedia.[1]) The seven parts include:

- Online marketplace services
- Broadband services
- Energy and commodities services
- Capital and risk management services
- Commercial and industrial outsourcing services project development and management services
- Energy transportation and upstream services

Given the scope of even this bare-bones list of the aspects of Enron's dealings, "That's a big list" comes to mind. How could any U.S. corporation, let alone in the world, have all the appropriate checks and balances in place to ensure that these subsidiaries and associated units were operating within proper corporate protocol and within legal limits? Simply put: They couldn't and they didn't. This scope of the business is actually part of how greed and corruption began to blossom within the company and led to its downfall. Looking back, it's no wonder Chanos looked at Enron and wondered why the company continued to acquire businesses, growing itself to such a size.

Until 1999–2000, Enron was essentially under the radar to the shorts. On the surface, the company appeared to be a profit behemoth, always growing and expanding coupled with a stock price that kept soaring. In 1999, Enron was huge and led by five men;

- Kenneth Lay, founder, chairman, and CEO
- Jeffrey Skilling, president, COO (later CEO for a few months in 2001)
- Andrew Fastow, CFO
- Lou Pai, CEO of Enron Energy Services
- Timothy Belden, head of trading at Enron Energy Services

These five men made up the core problem at Enron: greed. Hundreds of others can be implicated in this story, of course, but most of them are merely passing characters. Jeff Skilling was the mastermind of Enron's trading unit, and Lou Pai was his man in charge of its operation. Enron Energy Services reaped huge profits through complex derivatives trading of energy. Under Pai was Tim Belden, the head of trading, and Belden was responsible for strategies that brought California to its knees.

Off to the side, but certainly not in the shadows, was CFO Andy Fastow. A handsome man with a mischievous grin, Fastow helped Enron create dozens of shell companies, offshore entities, and special investment vehicles (SIVs) to help create false profits, offload Enron debt, and fool investors. And of course, Ken Lay, the CEO, was the mastermind who kept all the parts of the show going for years.

Jim Chanos says a friend alerted him to Enron's irregular accounting practices in 2000. In our interview, he related the following story:

*A catalyst for our involvement was simply a phone call I got from a friend in Dallas who ran a hedge fund who asked if I had seen the*

*Texas* Wall Street Journal *"Heard on the Street" column. . . . if I had heard about the accounting of the energy merchant banks. And I told him I hadn't seen it.*

*So he faxed it to me— e-mail was still not ubiquitous at that point—and it was a really interesting column about how the energy merchant banks had lobbied the SEC successfully for getting mark-to-model and mark-to-market accounting for their longterm investing in energy derivatives. To take the present value of all the future profits that were written into the derivatives were sold as opposed to adjusting it pro-rata over the life of the contract. And, uh, they were celebrating.*

*The article if I recall went on to say that there were a number of academics and accountants who were worried about this practice. That anytime you could front-load profits you'd really suspect that company of corporate abuse. We had had experience with this in a number of areas in the first subprime fiasco in the mid-'90s and then way, way back going back to the annuity issuers—Baldwin United and others—back in the early 1980s. They were selling insurance policies and cooking up all their future assumed income up front.*

*So immediately we became a little interested because over and over we've seen at the hands of unscrupulous management that kind of ability to in effect create instant profits by doing what were ultimately bad business deals just too lucrative to give up, and we basically started analyzing Enron right then and there, which was the October/November 2000 time frame.*

*We pulled the 1999 10-K and 10-Qs and immediately there were red flags all over the place. You know, there was the odd disclosure about the offshore entities that were set to do business with Enron.*

The offshore entities Chanos refers to included firms created by CFO Andy Fastow to funnel money to and from Enron. They carried names like "JLM II" and "Raptor." The problem with these entities was that they often, if not always, had a senior Enron executive (in many cases, Fastow himself) as the managing partner. In short, there was a huge conflict of interest. If a manager in the upper echelon of Enron's overall management is also managing a fund, firm, or company that is connected to Enron as a subsidiary, it is impossible to meet the fiduciary duties of both companies.

Chanos discussed Enron's accounting, which was a focal point for Kynikos Associates and their investigations into the company stock:

*There are other odd things that didn't get as much subsequent press. For example, we saw a violation of the matching policy under GAAP, which is when in the merchant banking operations, they would sell assets for a gain and it would be above the line as merchant banking income. But when they sold something at a reasonable loss they moved it into discontinued operations and then when they sold it, they put a loss on sale of discontinued operations. So, as opposed to booking both their profits AND their losses, they were putting it below the line so the analyst was disregarding it. . . .*

*The next thing that caught our eye, was even with what looked to be some pretty aggressive accounting, we calculated the company's pretax return on capital including their derivatives book to be somewhere a little north of 6 percent but below 7 percent. And based on what Enron bonds were trading at and the equity risk premium, we realized this company wasn't earning its cost of capital.*

*So it was a giant leveraged hedge fund, as my partner Doug Melen said at the time, that was earning 6 percent a year, if you would, on a leveraged balance sheet and you were gonna pay 6 to 10 times book for it. It made no sense.*

*Then finally, there were the more interesting secondary issues like the insider selling through 2000. [There were] a lot of executive departures in 2000.*

The uncovering of these types of red flags was all it took. In November 2000, Chanos's Kynikos Associates initiated a short position in Enron and Chanos's firm confidently placed its bet. The research had been done, and the evidence had been uncovered and was right in front of them. All that was left was to watch as Enron started its implosion.

## THE BEST POSITION

From November 1, 2000, to December 2001, Enron's stock price went from the mid-$70s to almost zero. That is all in just one year. Jeffery Skilling resigned on August 14, 2001, and it represented the final nail in

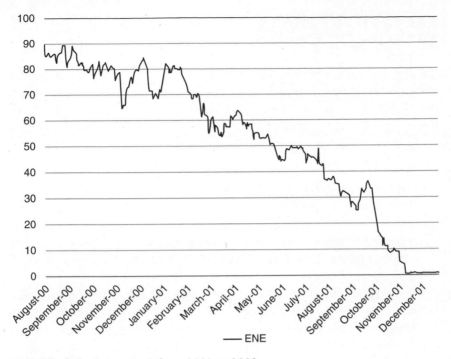

**FIGURE 2.1**  Enron Stock from 2000 to 2002
*Source:* Wikimedia Commons

the coffin and secured Enron's fate as a corrupt corporate empire on the brink of failure. Figure 2.1 depicts how quickly the price of Enron's stock fell.

Then, on December 2, 2001, just 13 months after Chanos had gone short, Enron filed for Chapter 11 bankruptcy protection. The game was up. Ken Lay, Andy Fastow, and Jeff Skilling would all go down with the ship in America's largest corporate bankruptcy. The total profit reaped by Kynikos Associates from its short position in Enron is estimated to have totaled around $500 million. Chanos became one of the best (and well-known, given the high visibility of the case) investors in the world.

Enron also left hundreds of people without jobs or retirement funds and garnered various law firms millions of dollars in legal fees. Looking back, it is incredible that such an opportunity to short a firm like Enron ever existed, but as a trader, one cannot help but wonder if a similar opportunity of epic proportions could arise again.

## RECREATING CHANOS'S TRADING STRATEGIES

Chanos has had many excellent strokes of luck and genius in his lengthy career speculating. His unique ability to comb through data and pick up on things that other traders don't notice is what makes him one of the best. Focusing primarily on the Enron trade, we can use Chanos's ideals and tactics to find similar opportunities on our own. To start, here are a few things to make a priority:

- Find companies where something about them just doesn't seem quite right. Maybe it clashes with your trading ideals.
- Watch out for companies with insanely overpriced stocks, a key give-away. While other companies may not be as corrupt as Enron was, you can look for the discrepancies and ask yourself why X company's stock is trading at Y price.
- Once you think you have found a company that is worth shorting, make sure you follow every tidbit of news about it, *especially SEC filings*. Also try creating Google Alerts (http://alerts.google.com) that will notify you when there's breaking news on the company.

## A MORE RECENT EXAMPLE

An example of a recent Enron-like collapse that ended in scandal, a huge loss of jobs and money, and a big ol' bankruptcy is Lehman Brothers. Enron was at one point the largest U.S. bankruptcy ever, but it was surpassed by Worldcom (2002), Washington Mutual (2008), and General Motors (2009). In September 2008, Lehman Brothers Holdings Inc. took the number one spot for largest U.S. bankruptcy.

Figure 2.2 depicts how Lehman Brothers's stock took a nosedive similar to that of Enron's. Also similar was how early warning signs (like off-balance sheet vehicles) revealed the true condition of Lehman's balance sheet leading up to its demise as part of the recent financial crisis.

If you paid attention to Lehman Brothers before the financial crisis and saw the company for what it truly was, you could have shorted Lehman stock (or, if you were an institutional investor, you could have entered into credit default swaps on Lehman debt). Either way, a fortune was waiting to be made—just like Chanos did with Enron.

The issue with finding opportunities such as these when you are a speculator is that they are becoming less commonplace. One could argue that

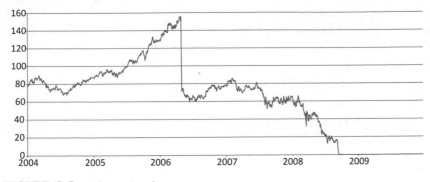

**FIGURE 2.2** Lehman Stock
*Source:* Historical data from Yahoo! Finance

regulators are more on top of today's markets and that businesses are required to be more transparent.

However, a trade that arose out of similar corruption was Tyco International. Tyco was embroiled in a huge legal battle stemming from a mergers and acquisitions spree that saw the company's credit rating drop in addition to its stock price. During the downfall, it was discovered that former chief executive officer Dennis Kozlowski had spent company money on a very lavish lifestyle. His spending eventually led to a class-action lawsuit and nearly destroyed the company. Tyco is another company Chanos shorted and made a nifty profit from in the process.

Figure 2.3 shows how similarly Tyco's stock acted to Lehman's once the cat was out of the bag. Clearly, Kozlowski's acquisition strategy did not bode well for the company. Shorting the stock at $55 a share and buying

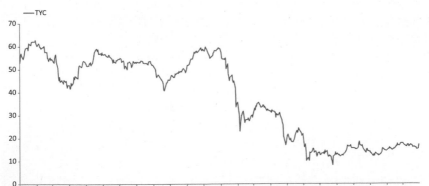

**FIGURE 2.3** Tyco Stock
*Source:* Historical data from Yahoo! Finance

to cover at $13 or $14 would have made for an excellent trade. While I'm not exactly sure of Chanos's entry and exit points on Tyco, the argument can be made that he probably did something similar to what he did with the Enron deal.

## CHANOS'S TOP TRAITS

To be a great short seller like Chanos, there are two key traits you can work on incorporating into your trading routines:

1. *Know your research abilities:* Chanos possesses great abilities to spot fraudulent companies before everyone else. How? He is a sleuth. Dive into a company's financial statements and SEC filings and dig until you find a footnote buried at the bottom with the information no one was supposed to see.

2. *Do what you know:* Chanos is a short seller (not exclusively, of course, but it is what he is best at). So, if you're good at trading futures, stick to futures. If distressed debt is your thing, then roll with it. Going into asset classes or sectors that are not your forte can lead to trouble.

■ ■ ■

Next up, you will learn about a legend in the global macro trading world, Paul Tudor Jones.

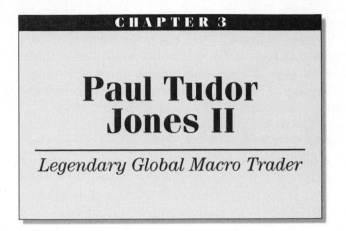

CHAPTER 3

# Paul Tudor Jones II

*Legendary Global Macro Trader*

P aul Tudor Jones has become the epitome of what people think of when they hear the words "Wall Street trader." Intense, brilliant, and sophisticated, Jones has built a personal fortune of $6 billion while returning untold fortunes to his investors.

Jones believes the key to successful trading is "an indefatigable and undying and unquenchable thirst for information and knowledge." Jones built a career upon this principle—always trying to understand the underlying psychological motives of all of the actors in what is a complex and endlessly dynamic marketplace. Although this philosophy would seem to be a standard on Wall Street, the actual method he used in practice tended against conventional wisdom.

## FOLLOWING A GENIUS

It is 4:00 A.M. on a Tuesday in the town of Greenwich, Connecticut. Most people here are soaking up their remaining hours of sleep before venturing out on a short commute into Manhattan to start their day running the corporations that have made New York City famous. Paul Tudor Jones is an entirely different story. While many of his colleagues sleep, Jones is already in his home office, where he has been on the phone for 45 minutes.

Although the Chicago Mercantile Exchange (CME) is still asleep, the trading day at the Hong Kong Mercantile Exchange (HKMEx) is coming to a crescendo. Jones is on the phone with an associate in the middle of the action there, who is relaying every one of the legendary money manager's bids into the marketplace. Jones is acting on new information that he has received about globally traded gold futures, and he knows that if he doesn't act now, he won't have long before his colleagues arriving in their New York offices take the opportunity out from under him.

Finally, getting the position that he wanted, Jones rushes into his office to be greeted by some of the first-arriving analysts. The commute is short—the headquarters of Tudor Investment Corporation is only a few miles from his palatial estate in Greenwich—and from the moment he arrives, Jones is extremely animated. Although he is calm and collected while discussing economic matters with his employees, Jones' demeanor changes dramatically as soon as he gets on the phone. His voice becomes frantically urgent, yelling out orders to his brokers as his advisors feed him information. He realizes that with each trade, he puts millions of his investors' dollars on the line.

His office is adorned with the unassuming furniture, generic artwork, and fluorescent lighting panels that one might associate with a low-budget sales operation. As he sits down at his desk, he is surrounded by his small, surprisingly young team of economic advisors who are ready with any type of analysis that the master investor might need in order to decide which trades are worth taking during the course of the trading day. A self-proclaimed global macro trader, Jones needs access to all types of financial and economic data and analysis from anywhere around the world on the fly.

It has been the routine for Jones since his career began.

## THE PATH OF GREATNESS

Unlike many of the traders mentioned in this book, Jones found success very early in his career. Shortly after graduating from college, he took a job at the New York Cotton Exchange and soon afterward was introduced to Eli Tullis, who would become his mentor. During those early years, he formulated many of the principles that would define his trading strategies for the rest of his illustrious career.

From the beginning, Jones was extraordinarily confident in his ability to read the future of the marketplace. Despite all of the profitable bets that he placed in his early work, the investment that most impacted his career was in 1979 when he lost 60 to 70 percent of his equity in a single trade on the New York Cotton Exchange. Although it was before he started his own fund, he had already built a successful career on the trading floor. To this day, he says that it was his overconfidence in his abilities that led him to take such a dramatic loss, which is why he now is much less cocksure with his investment strategies.

During the 1980s and 1990s, Jones was a fixture on the Wall Street social scene and wasn't shy about enjoying his wealth. In 1987 alone, he made $80 million to $100 million—enough money to have every urge met as a 30-something New Yorker. His personality and trading philosophy was chronicled in the 1987 PBS film *TRADER: The Documentary*. The film shows Jones predicting the 1987 crash using forecasting techniques we'll talk about in this chapter. The intensity and commitment displayed by Jones in the documentary is awe inspiring. He lives, eats, and breathes fund management and expects no less from those who surround him. It is somewhat comical to see Jones using technology that today is all but useless. For instance, in the documentary, one scene depicts Jones leaning over a brand-new printer that was custom designed to create time-series charts. Although this job is now easily completed by a few keystrokes in Excel, Jones used this cutting-edge technology (at the time) to gain a foothold on the marketplace.

Indeed, according to many of the financiers who have known and worked with him over the years, Jones has always been on the cutting edge. Many traders who were with him in that era have said that his ideas were 20 years ahead of the rest of the marketplace.

Although the documentary was broadcast on public-access television, it has largely been removed from circulation. Jones has become far more reserved in recent years and is reportedly embarrassed by the his former swaggering demeanor. To this end, Jones and his lawyers have spent a great deal of money in an attempt to erase the documentary from memory. Despite their efforts, it has found a strong cult following among aspiring Wall Street traders, who pay large amounts of money for a copy of the rare film.

## Starting Out

Jones's path of greatness began in 1975 during his senior year of college at the University of Virginia when a friend described trading to him as "the most challenging game that you can play."

Since childhood, Jones had an extremely competitive yet sociable personality. In college, Jones fostered these traits by joining a fraternity and participating in team-oriented sports and activities. He applied his spirit to boxing, becoming a welterweight champion. His classmates remember his competitive spirit; he was always confident in his abilities, even when faced with an insurmountable challenge. These traits would serve him well in later years. As any financial analyst knows, it is often impossible to identify a profitable position with mathematical certainty. The financial system is large and complex, and potential investment opportunities can often be debated from several angles. However, Jones's intensity and confidence allowed him to forge on with financial strategies, even when his positions were contrary to conventional wisdom. He soon realized that his competitive advantage was his ability to meld instinct with sound analysis.

Shortly after finishing his degree in economics, Jones started working as a clerk on the floor of the New York Cotton Exchange. Jones's competitive spirit thrust him almost immediately into the spotlight, and he soon became a broker for the highly respected firm E. F. Hutton & Co. It was a perfect match, and he became an avid student of the commodity markets. The intensity of the trading floor, when combined with his unforgiving competitive nature, propelled Jones to success.

Because he found such quick success when starting out, he became extremely confident in his split-second investment abilities. But one day in 1979, during an intense session in the cotton futures market, Jones nearly burned out. Bidding ranged from 82 to 86 cents per contract. Although Jones already had a sizable long position, an act of sheer bravado led him to bid 82.90 for 100 July contracts. Mishearing the bid, Jones's broker offered 90 for 100 July, which was almost instantly bought up by an eager counterparty. In an instant, Jones had mistakenly bet the farm—making him long a total of 600 contracts—a gigantic position for the time. Realizing that the market was about to turn down to 78 cents, Jones began to sell, but his position was so large that it took several days to dump.

In that single trade, Jones's clients lost between 60 and 70 percent of their equity. Despite the long-term value that he knew he had been bringing to these investors, this catastrophe demoralized him, leading him to seriously consider leaving the fund management world behind. Somehow he found the strength to go on and continued his career, but he would always remember that day and how unforgiving the market is of arrogance.

In 1980, Jones broke away from the firm to start working on his own. For two and a half years, he was extremely successful and was, as he has put it, "printing money every month." But despite the financial rewards, the young Jones felt unfulfilled. He applied to Harvard Business School and was accepted. As he prepared to move to Boston, though, Jones began to think there might be a better place for him to gain the type of experience that he was looking for while still allowing him to fulfill his need to socialize. Not wanting to make such a critical decision in haste, Jones consulted his cousin, William Dunavant, who at the time was a successful cotton merchant. On his advice, Jones spoke to Eli Tullis, a legendary commodities trader who would become his mentor. Tullis convinced Jones to return to the New York Cotton Exchange under his wing. With vigor, Jones soaked up the intensity and emotional disconnect demonstrated by his newfound guide.

He took away many important lessons from Tullis, including how trading a greater volume did not always lead to greater returns. With small position sizes, a trader can be mobile enough to exit the position at the right point. However, due to decreases in liquidity during market peaks and troughs, traders who possess large positions cannot exit a market until the market lets them out. This contrarian notion that larger funds are not necessarily better has stayed with Jones throughout his career, and has driven his philosophy to keep his fund as small as possible.

Over the next few years, Jones set off on his own again—this time with a larger team to help satisfy his need to socialize. In 1983, the Tudor Investment Corporation started in full swing, with a grand total of $300,000 under management. The new fund grew exponentially. By the late 1980s he had several hundred million dollars under management. His returns were exceptional. An investor with a share of his managed futures fund worth $1,000 in 1984 would be able to cash out for $17,482 only four years later. During the year of 1987 alone, Jones nearly tripled the fund, netting himself a personal payout of between $80 million and $100 million.

Remembering the advice on position sizes imparted to him by Tullis, Jones started to feel that his fund was getting too large to manage effectively, and he restricted the amount of new investment. However, due to his acumen, the fund continued to grow, surpassing $17 billion in 2007.

## KNOWING *All* THE MARKETS

Unlike many of the traders discussed in this book, Jones has never relied on long-shot investments with potentially gigantic returns in order to deliver results to his investors. While others traders (like George Soros, coming up in Chapter 7) sometimes take on incredibly risky positions based on only a hunch, Jones has always wanted to feel like he is in control of the financial well-being of his fund. His acumen relies on detailed technical and fundamental analyses, and he believes these are the cornerstone of *any* sound financial investment.

Jones has built a career of strong, long-term returns based on a set of principles he has developed to keep himself disciplined. Although he is extremely secretive. many of his principles can be inferred from his trades and the few interviews with him that have come to public light.

Jones adamantly supports the idea of removing the emotional connection between the trader and the marketplace. As any successful trader knows, having discipline is a critical component to success. It is extremely easy to get carried away with a market rally and ride past a predefined stop only to get caught in an illiquid position when the market turns around. Allowing your emotions to control your trading pattern leads to the logic behind your strategies becoming moot, and this can be disastrous.

Jones extends this removal of emotional connection to how he views his past decisions. As soon as a decision is made, it's in the past. He won't concentrate on a mistake that he made three seconds ago as much as what he is planning to do in the next move. This mantra allows him to act logically—like a computer algorithm—while maintaining the dynamic market intelligence that has made him such a dynamo investor.

In addition, many traders will analyze a single security as if it existed in a financial vacuum. This method makes it easy for traders to specialize in a specific type of asset—giving them the opportunity to focus their attention. Jones takes an entirely different approach. Knowing that the prices of many securities are interlinked, one of Jones's core competencies has always been his ability to make decisions based on his entire portfolio. Instead of waiting for idiosyncratic information to be released about individual assets, Jones looks for systematic trends that arise from anywhere in the global markets. This approach is the primary building block of his underlying methodology, which has become known as macro-level trading.

## Global Macro Trading

Jones is a self-proclaimed master of global macro trading—a set of strategies based on global macroeconomic conditions. Most investors concentrate on a small range of financial securities and analyze the factors that they believe influence the prices of those securities. Global macro (GMI) investors take a different approach.

First, GMI are interested in the movements of macroeconomic indicators and study how they might influence their positions. While a traditional equity trader might focus on how an earnings report from General Motors might affect their stake in the company, a global macro trader would take it a step further and look at unemployment numbers and GDP per capita. Also, global macro traders aren't bound by traditional marketplaces. A critical part of their strategy is based on how international prices might influence one another. They therefore operate across international bounds.

Of all the hedge fund strategies discussed in this book, global macro managers have the largest variety of tools. Managers can take a position in practically any market or instrument in the world, giving them access to strategies not available to more traditional funds. The position taken by a GMI fund manager is generally classified into two categories:

1. A directional position is when a manager bets on price movements of a single currency, such as if they were to take a long position on the U.S. dollar if they thought that it was undervalued.

2. They can take a position on the relative value, where they believe that two securities are mispriced in relation to each other, which would entail a long-position in one security and a short-position in another.

Global macro trading has been an extraordinarily profitable means of managing money. Between 1990 and 2005, global macro hedge funds have posted an average annualized return of over 15 percent. Jones fully uses global macro strategies. This gives him the opportunity to have a much greater breadth when attempting to identify the mispricing of securities.

Jones's overarching strategy also involves an understanding of market cycles. The majority of trading strategies involve predicting long-term market trends. During both bearish and bullish markets, it can be difficult for investors to imagine that prices will soon turn around. People tend to get stuck in their models and assume that current conditions will persist in order to align with the fundamental analysis that they have conducted. Jones's strategy, however, shows us that he knows that markets are in flux most of the time. This tenet has led Jones to base his investment decisions on his own predictions of market swings. The most interesting facet of this approach is how Jones actually went about predicting turns.

During the 1980s, a relatively new form of financial analysis became wildly popular. These techniques, collectively known as technical analysis, use the historical price information of stocks in order to predict their future values. See Figure 3.1 for a simple example of this new wave of financial modeling.

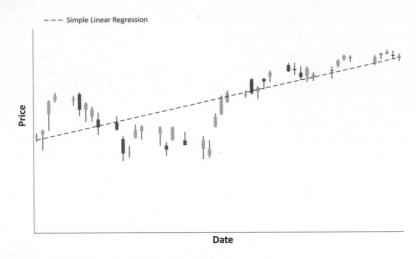

**FIGURE 3.1**   Example of Technical Analysis
*Source:* Historical data from Yahoo! Finance

The majority of traders using technical analysis methods will look at a trend of past performance and draw out where they think that prices will go. The type of analysis shown in Figure 3.1 is only a simple linear regression, but many traders use far more intricate models using high-level statistics and even stochastic calculus. Jones's model was a bit more involved than the basic methods because he also used a methodology known as Elliot wave theory.

Elliot wave theory suggests that markets move in cycles that are extremely predictable due to several somewhat pedantic psychological components of trading. Extending the principles involved, Jones took market data from the present and correlated it against historical data from the overarching market. He extrapolated a time period with a high correlation and began making investments as if he were living in the past with a roadmap to the future.

His combined technique—Elliot wave regression— proved wildly successful. The marketplace tended to continue along the predetermined path, and his analysis eventually allowed him to predict the 1987 market crash.

## Elliot Wave Theory

It is commonly accepted that the economy operates on a continual cycle. When a market enters a trough, assets are priced below their fundamental values due to the expectation of further downturn. As soon as investors believe that the markets have bottomed out, capital begins to flow into underpriced securities, pushing their prices up. As the market rallies, more and more investors invest in these assets, pushing the price into a bull market. Eventually, these investors overextend their capital and push the price above a sustainable level. When the market realizes that it has become overpriced, investors quickly dump their positions, causing prices to crash down in a bear market move to another trough. This process is commonly accepted by market participants, but Jones takes it a step further by additionally using Elliot wave theory.

Elliot wave theory is the belief in overarching market cycles. The largest cycles, known as grand supercycles, can last for hundreds of years. The current grand supercycle is thought to have begun when America declared independence from Great Britain in 1776. Each cycle is made up of many smaller, yet equally predictable cycles. Within a grand supercycle, there is a supercycle, lasting between 40 and 70 years. Smaller still is a cycle, lasting one to several years. This process continues down to cycles that last only a matter of minutes. Figure 3.2 illustrates this theory.

During the 1980s, Jones ran a series of correlation analyses that led him to believe that the market was following a similar pattern as the bull market in the 1920s. Indeed, when the two trend charts are put side by side, a correlation of over 90 percent emerges—which Jones thought as too extraordinary to happen by chance.

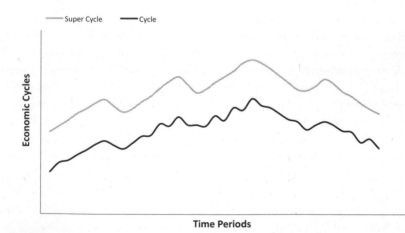

**FIGURE 3.2**   Elliot Wave Theory
*Source:* Created with theoretical data

One of the most phenomenal affirmations of the efficacy of this method came in February 1987. The market had bet against the Dow Jones index. However, Jones—in accordance with the predictions made by the corresponding trend lines of the 1920s—took on dramatic long positions. His bet paid off, and he made close to $5 million for his firm in a single day. Before the year was out, his model would predict an opposite market swing—a crash that would rival the Great Depression.

Jones was able to predict the 1987 crash to practically the day. He took on huge short positions based on this methodology and ended up nearly tripling the value of his fund in a very short period of time.

## MORE KEYS TO JONES'S SUCCESS

When Jones launched his fund, he knew that he wanted to take a different approach. At the time, most people took on long-term positions which were designed to take advantage of stocks as they trended up or down and make money throughout the overall cycle of a stock. However, Jones discovered that stocks would steadily trend during only about 15 percent of their lifecycle. During the rest of the time, stocks would move back and forth between high and low prices. Jones became an expert at predicting these swings.

In particular, Jones used his analysis techniques to pinpoint the top and bottom of cycles in order to exploit them for his fund. He has admitted that he has probably lost many opportunities by not taking advantage of trending stocks, however; when markets exhibit reversals, traders often overreact. Knowing this, Jones takes advantage of the emotion tied up in the marketplace and is an expert at turning it into an advantage for his fund.

Jones hates the feeling of being uncomfortable with the position that he has taken. He never bets on a security in front of key reports that he has no control over—which equates to, in his mind, common betting. This leads into one of his key traits—he never likes to lose money. Most investors understand that a down month or two can be a key component of an overall successful strategy. It is often necessary to try new things in the market, and failure offers a springboard from which to learn what actually works. Jones has never agreed with that mantra. He views every day of investing as a totally new start. His goal is to end the day with more money in his accounts than when the day started. By his own account, this makes him perhaps "the single most conservative investor on earth."

Although Jones purports to know exactly when market turnarounds will occur, there has always been a quiet, persistent voice in the back of his head saying that the marketplace is a completely unpredictable animal. He has always had a constant aversion to having his wealth tied up to the marketplace. As he put it in an interview:

> *My grandfather told me at a very early age that you are only worth what you can write a check for tomorrow, so the concept of having my net worth tied up in a stock a la Bill Gates [...] would be something that's just anathema to me.*"[1]

This is a key factor that has drawn Jones to the futures market. Liquidity in the futures market allows an investor to generally cash out their position in just a few minutes. This flexibility gives Jones the ability to quickly step back from the market when he is unsure as to its future direction.

One of the key lessons that Jones took away from his early mentor Eli Tullis was the now-common concept of the importance of position sizes. Although many fund managers will brag about the size of the fund they have under management, Jones knew it was important to keep these numbers close to his chest order to continue making returns also grow. Inevitably, these positions become unwieldy and immobile. Since the market has only a limited amount of liquidity, it becomes increasingly more difficult to exit a position at the exact right moment. A fund manager is therefore forced to exit the position over time as the price makes its way to the predicted inflection point. In effect, this relationship means that there is a threshold whereby afterward every additional dollar put into a fund reduces the ability of the fund manager to produce returns. Furthermore, there is a tendency for markets to naturally decrease in liquidity at the highs and lows of an economic cycle.

These market extremes are where Jones makes most of his trades, which further reduces the feasible size of the fund. This is why Jones has strived to keep his fund as small as possible. He stopped taking on new investors many years ago and will often return capital gains in order to reduce his position. However, even Jones admits that the money he manages has grown too large—perhaps he is too apt a fund manager for his own good.

Playing the market can make for an extraordinarily turbulent career. Although we all would like to be as cool, detached, and logical as some of the great traders during market fluctuations, the fact is that fortunes are made and lost during the ups and downs of stock prices. This causes many a would-be market guru to clench up and stop using his head. A critical component of Jones's success has been his ability to separate his emotions from his fund's performance. Although he knows that with each trade he puts a great deal of his own and his investors' money on the line, Jones knows that he must keep cool in order to ensure that he is making sound financial decisions. To accomplish this, he has had a long-standing guiding principle to "stay calm" irrespective of the situation in the marketplace. He avoids entering into positions that he feels uncomfortable with, and he quickly exits positions that he thinks might increase his exposure too much. He has never been a fan of taking on inordinate levels of risk and will constantly adjust his portfolio to match this aversion.

Jones has strict guidelines for how he is supposed to trade when he is trading. Although he likes to think that he remains logical in any situation, he knows that emotions always influence how decisions are made. To combat these natural tendencies, Jones defines his strategies before entering into positions. He writes down limits: points where he could automatically exit his position. This has stopped him from getting carried away and forces him to stick to his plan.

Even with these techniques, Jones has far from a perfect trading record. The systematic risk of the marketplace dictates that even the most apt trader will eventually lose out. Although many would let a losing bet affect their aversion to risk, Jones takes a much more level-headed approach. As soon as a trade is completed, he moves on. Whether he makes or loses money, there is no reason to dwell in the past.

In addition, above his office desk is a sign that says, "Never Average Losers." This slogan represents one of the key strategies that Jones relies on to continually make returns. While many fund managers "average down" (buying additional shares in a stock that you already own as its price slides down and selling them as it slides up), Jones does not because it essentially means that the average price paid for the stock will decrease as you buy more shares for less money. For example, if you have a position of 1,000 shares in IBM that you bought for $140 and the price drops to $130, you could buy 100 more shares, making the average cost per share only $139. As the share continues to decrease, the investor buys additional shares of the stock. The wisdom behind this strategy is that other investors are irrationally devaluing the stock and it will eventually revert to the mean.

Jones stays away from this cookie-cutter strategy, believing if a stock is heading downward there is no justification for blindly increasing the exposure. He doesn't stick with "loser" stocks. Instead, he sticks to his initial analysis for entering the position. If he believes that the stock is being undervalued, he might buy more shares but he will not let market swings alone dictate the overall strategy.

## SUCCESS BEYOND TRADING

Despite all of his financial success, Jones cites his wife and four children as his greatest success. Although there are definite business benefits of having your office in proximity to your home, Jones likely has an ulterior motive—he wants to spend as much time near his family as possible.

Jones has also done much more with his life than launching and growing his fund. Since the beginning, he has been conscious of the world around him, realizing that he has been extraordinarily lucky in his career, and has always strived to give back. Remembering the life-changing impact that he had while studying under his mentor, Eli Tullis, Jones has taken a great deal of up-and-coming traders under his wing. However, it has been with mixed results.

One important outreach program he finances is his I Have a Dream program, focusing on financing the college education of underprivileged teenagers from Brooklyn. He was drawn to the project because he felt that helping kids at such a young age would magnify the good done over their lifetime. The I Have a Dream program is part of a larger initiative called the Robin Hood Foundation (www.robinhood.org). As a founding partner, Jones set up this organization to deal directly with outside charitable enterprises in an attempt to cut out the middle man that is characteristic of the nonprofit industry. True to its name, the Robin Hood Foundation has long-term relationships with many of the nation's wealthiest families, who are looking to help their neighbors. The board of directors is composed of some of the most successful business leaders, lawyers, and community leaders in the country, who have collectively been extremely effective in helping working-class families live productive lives.

## RECREATING JONES'S TRADING STRATEGIES

Jones's brazen utilization of Elliot wave theory is legendary. Despite the knee-jerk reaction to discredit this strategy, Jones proved himself by making astronomical returns for his investors over a very long period. Indeed,

**FIGURE 3.3** Correlation
*Source:* Historical data from Yahoo! Finance

a comparison of the Dow Jones Industrial average between 1982 to 1986 and 1932 to 1936 (see Figure 3.3) shows striking similarities between the two periods. When the data is looked at on a daily basis (as Jones would have looked at it), the correlation is almost 93 percent!

Although the strategy makes sense in retrospect, it must have been extraordinarily difficult to remain faithful to at the time. It must have seemed as though the two periods were heavily diverging. For instance, by mid-1983, the bull market of the 1980s overtook the market of the early 1930s. The correlation of the two datasets up to this point was much smaller than the entire two periods, but Jones stuck to his guns. In the end, his strategy proved viable and he was able to return huge sums to his investors.

## JONES'S TOP TRAITS

Jones helped define the cliché Wall Street traits that much of the industry and its participants attempt to emulate today. Here are a just a few that you can learn from:

- *Intensity:* The intensity and dedication demonstrated by Jones in his trading is legendary. He was among the first on Wall Street to operate on a worldwide scale, waking up at 5 A.M. to talk with his people in London and catch the tail end of the trading day in China.

- *Keeping a comprehensive viewpoint:* When approaching the marketplace, Jones looks at how individual financial instruments affect the widespread economic and social fabric of a global landscape. Although it provides a challenge, Jones took it on headfirst. In an early application of financial chaos theory, Jones knew that the economy is far more complex than most analysts admit.
- *Having a methodical approach:* Despite Jones's admission of his own helplessness when approaching the market, he has been extremely good at sticking to the few core principles in this chapter.

■ ■ ■

Paul Tudor Jones approaches trading like a pure science. His dedication, acumen, and core principles have allowed him to become one of the legends of Wall Street. Hard working and intense, Jones still wakes up at the crack of dawn in order to follow the markets and create macro-level trading opportunities. Although he has become less active in recent years, the work that he was involved with while he built up his fund fundamentally changed the way that fund managers handle financial analysis. His global outlook came at a time when most firms concentrated on a small basket of securities with a limited scope. Jones brought forth the fact that financial products the world over are interlinked and that there is an undeniable profit to be made from exploiting these connections.

Amazingly self-confident even today, Jones keeps around 85 percent of his net worth tied to his fund, which he says is the "safest place in the world for it." In his mind, he will always be a trader—even when he retires from his fund.

Next, you will learn about legendary mutual fund manager John Templeton.

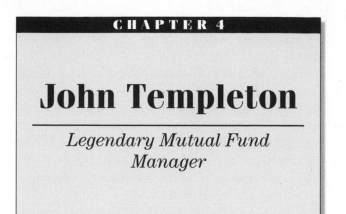

## CHAPTER 4

# John Templeton

*Legendary Mutual Fund Manager*

J ohn Templeton was a simple, even-tempered gentleman with a sunny disposition and a heart of gold. Growing up in a small town in southern Tennessee, he found a deep devotion to religion.

Unlike many fund managers, Templeton did not choose a career in trading to make money for himself. Instead, he saw managing a mutual fund as helping other people to responsibly invest in themselves and their financial future. He saw himself as a saint whose job it was to help the huddled masses of the world—and he did a lot to further that cause.

Templeton launched and grew one of the largest, most successful mutual funds of the 20th century. His levelheadedness and thrift while investing allowed him maximize net returns for his shareholders without wasting earnings on normal corporate inefficiencies. And although his family is now largely divested from the fund, the fund has become a force in the financial world with over $29 billion under management.

If asked, Templeton would undoubtedly cite his ability to bootstrap his businesses for the benefit of shareholders as his primary competitive advantage. In each of his offices, he operated with the bare minimum of luxuries, using only what was essential for his operation's survival.

## WHAT MADE TEMPLETON FAMOUS

Templeton's thriftiness in investing was obvious even in his teen years. When he was only 12 years old, Templeton decided that he wanted to have his own car. In 1924, he went out and found a great bargain—an old Ford that a farmer was willing to part with for only $10. However, there was a problem with the classic car; very few of its parts worked. In order to fix his new car, the young Templeton went out and found an identical car that was also priced at $10. Over the next several months, Templeton and his friends set to work on the two vehicles, swapping parts back and forth, using tools borrowed from their fathers and technical guides borrowed from a mechanic. Soon, one of the old cars was running, and it cost them only their $20. Templeton had this first car until giving it up before college. His ability to make something out of nothing was a major driving force in how he conducted business for the rest of his life.

Unlike Bass and Jones, profiled earlier, Templeton generally had very few individual trades with huge returns. Instead, he was an avid proponent of long-term, slow-growing investments derived from sound fundamental analysis and traditional portfolio management. Early in his career, though, he did have one trade that he would become well known for.

In 1939, the world was spiraling into a second world war. Europe degraded under the iron fist of Nazi fascists, and the global financial markets held their breath. To make matters worse, the United States was on the tail end of the Great Depression. The stock market was in shambles. However, Templeton knew that all of these factors, when combined, could spell positive future returns in the stock market. It seemed like the perfect storm, and all Templeton could see was the silver lining. He knew from his studies of historical financial markets that a world war would increase the need for goods more than during peacetime. Even inefficient and poorly managed companies would soon see a dramatic spike in demand. Templeton bought $100 of each stock that was trading for less than $1. This was a risky trade at the time: 37 of the 104 companies that were part of his trade had already declared some form of bankruptcy. But after only four years, Templeton's investment quadrupled in value and, surprisingly, only four of the overall investments ended up being worthless. See Figure 4.1 for an overview of the market during the Great Depression.

Although this trade was one of the most risky Templeton would enact in his career, it would teach him two important lessons:

1. Had he kept his investments for longer, he would have made even more profit. This added fuel to his belief that long-term positions far outweigh the benefits of short-term ones.

2. This trade helped him develop his theory of the "point of greatest pessimism." As mentioned previously, the combination of the Great

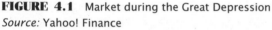

**FIGURE 4.1** Market during the Great Depression
*Source:* Yahoo! Finance

Depression and the breakout of World War II had created an extremely unfriendly environment for investing. The idea of investing any amount into firms that appeared to be on the edge of failure was unimaginable, let alone basing an entire strategy on such a move. Templeton used this zeitgeist of the point of greatest pessimism as an inflection point in the marketplace: when the financial industry is reluctant to enter into a position because of the risk, Templeton knows it's time to buy

Templeton used these two lessons throughout his career and in investments spanning the world, but perhaps never in such a dramatic fashion as during World War II.

## TEMPLETON'S LIFE BEFORE INVESTING

John Templeton's grandfather, Dr. John Wiley Templeton, practiced medicine for 40 years. He was a trained field surgeon in the Confederate army during the Civil War and remained devoutly committed to the confederacy for the rest of his life. After retiring, Dr. Templeton moved to Winchester, Tennessee, to be closer to his son Harvey and Harvey's wife, Vella Handly, who would go on to raise one of the greatest investors of the 20th century.

Templeton always loved the house that his father, Harvey, had built for Vella right down the street from his grandparents. It was a small brick house on six acres, with one acre dedicated to his mother's flower garden. Templeton's father had a business building houses, and he spent most of his summers helping him lay wire in his new houses. He grew up interested in everything to do with working with his hands. His father was also involved in the cotton business in the 1920s. At $2 per bale, the Templeton's cotton gin would often process more than 2,000 bales of cotton per season.

All of Harvey's businesses provided a very comfortable lifestyle for the young John Templeton. Although he would never reach the same level as affluence as his son, Harvey provided Templeton with the life lessons which shaped his investing career.

Templeton was extremely proud of his genealogical connections to the Old South. His mother was the daughter of a prominent businessman, Robert Clinton Handly, who owned an extremely profitable grain mill. In turn, Robert was a direct descendant of Samuel Handly, who had been a war hero during the Revolutionary War. Templeton's maternal grandmother, Elizabeth Marks, was the sister of Colonel Albert Marks, who had been a governor of Tennessee.

Templeton was also brought up in a very religious household, and he used his parents' teachings on doing the work of God throughout his career. Even after his fund grew into a world-class institution, Templeton began every investor meeting with prayer. Although some might see asking God for material gains as sacrilegious, Templeton claimed that he would use prayer as a form of meditation—to induce a calm, collective consciousness among his investors and employees. Later in his career, Templeton founded the John Templeton Prize, which was awarded to an individual who had furthered the interests of religion during a given year.

## Educational Aspirations

Templeton had an adventurous childhood. He and his brother Harvey had free reign to explore the world. Templeton excelled at school and decided to attend college. He wanted to attend Yale University but had to take a test given by the College Entrance Examination Board (CEEB) as well as meet stringent subject requirements. However, nobody at his high school had ever taken the CEEB, and a few of the requisite subjects were not taught. Templeton ended up sending away for copies of the CEEB tests from the previous several years and used the tests to study for the examination every summer throughout high school.

Despite his academic prowess, Templeton was not a nerd. He had a well-rounded life and hung out with girls, went to dances, and played football during high school, and his hard work and well-roundedness paid off. Templeton graduated at the top of his class in 1930 and was accepted into Yale, becoming the first student from his high school to go to college.

That year, 1930, was not a good year for the rest of the country. Following the stock market crash of 1929, the world was spiraling down into the Great Depression. Even back then, Ivy League tuition was a financial burden but Templeton's parents had saved a modest fund for each of their children's educations. To shore up that money, he happily worked several summer jobs, including selling newspapers door to door. Templeton was already a keen businessperson but, despite his success, selling goods door to door never sat right with him. He didn't like the concept of trying to force people to buy goods they didn't need. This early experience contributed to the goals he made for his fund later in his career.

When Templeton arrived at Yale, he was out of his element. The majority of his classmates had attended privately-run college preparatory schools in the northeast and many were already friends before they arrived on campus. By the beginning of the second year, though, Templeton's affable nature started to win him a group of friends. In the meantime, his father broke the news to him that he could no longer contribute money toward his tuition because of the financial constraints of the Great Depression. Templeton was devastated, but upon returning to college he applied for every scholarship and grant. The university helped him find work and he scraped by. Templeton studied very hard to keep his scholarships, and by the end of his third year he had become the top student in his class. His prowess earned him the presidency of Phi Beta Kappa, an academic honors society. Additionally, he joined Elihu, a senior society, and was the business manager of a comic magazine.

During his final year at Yale, Templeton served as senior aide at Pierson College, guiding students in the same financial situation that he had been in. He applied for the Rhodes scholarship offered by Yale and, after an extremely competitive process, was chosen as one of only two students from his region to win. During the following two years at Oxford, Templeton was unable to study business or economics since they were not yet offered, but he would return years later to help found Oxford's first management school: Templeton College, named after Templeton himself.

During his time at Oxford, Templeton traveled extensively during vacation periods. After graduating, he convinced a classmate to accompany him on a 35-country, seven-month trip around the world. The plan was to spend as little as possible, and in the end, their trip cost them less than $200. Living among impoverished people around the world in that time taught Templeton lifelong lessons on how most of the world's people make it through their daily lives. The trip solidified his desire to launch a career in investing, and the experiences he had during his travels were a critical component of the development of his perspective on worldwide markets. Even in his youth, he had a keen understanding of the complex financial markets, which would help build the rest of his career.

## The Married Life

In 1937, when Templeton returned home from traveling, he married Judith Dudley Folk, a girl who had been his summer love and secret fiancé for three years. Dudley, who liked to be known by her middle name, had gone to Wellesley College but spent summers at her family's vacation home in the mountains of Tennessee. The wedding was a major event in Nashville society, with newspapers full of the beautiful dinners and garden parties that composed the wedding extravaganza. After being married, Templeton whisked Dudley off to Mexico City for their two-week honeymoon, after which they drove to New York to start their careers.

Before going on his previous international adventures, Templeton had sent out a hundred letters to brokerage houses, financial advisories, and investment banks outlining his background and asking to be considered for a permanent position. He was offered an interview at twelve investment firms. After a rigorous interview process, five companies offered him a position. Templeton took a job at Fenner & Beane for $150 per month. Although it was not the highest paid of his offers, Templeton believed that it was the greatest opportunity to learn. However, Templeton's tenure at F&B was short-lived. After three months of living in New York, a fellow Rhodes scholar, George McGhee, helped Templeton to get a job working with him as the secretary-treasurer of the National Geophysical Company, which was a firm focused on seismograph exploration. George talked his boss, William Salvatori, into offering Templeton $350 per month to coax him to move to Texas.

With an offer that would double his salary, Templeton discussed moving with Dudley, who had found a job working for Young & Rubicam, an advertising agency in the Chrysler Building. Although she was happy with her $150 per month, she had already grown tired of working for a big firm and welcomed the change in scenery. While in Texas, Dudley opened up her own advertising agency.

The Templetons lived in Texas for two years and saved every possible penny of his paycheck. His long-term goal was to save 50 percent of his net salary so he and Dudley could move back to New York and he could start his own investment advisory firm. He and Dudley played games searching for the best bargains on their everyday purchases. They would set unrealistically low budgets and through hard work and ingenuity somehow meet their goals. For instance, to furnish their first five-bedroom apartment in New York, they budgeted only $25. They then attended auctions held by people who were moving out of the city and focused on unclaimed items. They bought chairs for 10 cents and coffee tables for 25 cents. Their biggest splurge by far was a $200 sofa bed that they bought for $5.

## TEMPLETON'S BIG MOVE

During the first half of 1939, the political climate of Europe had declined to an unsustainable level. In September 1939, Germany invaded Poland. Although the United States would not engage in conflict for another three years, it was obvious to Templeton that a second world war had begun.

Templeton knew that during times of great conflict, practically every commodity and product is suddenly in extraordinary demand regardless of price. He took this analysis to mean that even companies that were inefficiently run and might not survive in a normal economic climate would thrive. In order to bet on his analysis, Templeton departed from his normal debt-free mantra and borrowed $10,000 from Dick Platt, his former boss at Fenner & Beane, and bought $100 of every stock that was selling for less than a dollar. Prior to making this trade, Templeton's investment portfolio totaled around $30,000.

Templeton's move was not without risk. As mentioned at the beginning of this chapter, 37 of the 104 companies which he bought a stake in that fall were currently undergoing bankruptcy proceedings. However, the dramatic increase in wartime manufacturing turned most of those companies around and, within four years, Templeton sold off all the investments. His $10,000 investment was worth $40,000.

Although he had made a great deal of money through this deal, Templeton always wished he had stayed in longer. Although many of the stocks he held tripled in value, many became worth over a hundred times what Templeton originally paid for them. This experience shaped much of his future fund management activities. He developed the idea that real money was made by taking long-term, safe positions and letting compounding returns grow money without intervention. This concept of letting money work for him was perhaps the driving inspiration of his subsequent career. From an early stage, he was enthralled with the idea that capital gains from one year built upon the profits from previous years.

## Back to New York

A year after he and Dudley had moved back to New York, Templeton launched his own firm. With savings in hand, he found an opportunity to join George Towne, an investment advisor with only eight clients, and help him take his company to the next level. Templeton offered him $5,000 to take over the operation, and the name of the company became Towne, Templeton & Dobbrow. A short time after, the firm merged with Vance, Chapin & Company to become Templeton, Dobbrow & Vance.

During the first few years, Templeton rarely took a salary. Relying on his savings, he was wholeheartedly focused on making money for his investors, and he built much of the firm on the principle of being extremely careful with money. After realizing that most office equipment lost a great deal of value after being used, he instituted a policy of rarely buying anything new, finding, for example, typewriters that were only a few months old at a 40 percent discount. He also applied this principle to office space. After having an office in Manhattan proved to be too expensive, he found a space above a drugstore near his home in Englewood, New Jersey. Because it was in an old building in disrepair, Templeton was able to rent all 2,000 feet of office space for only about $160 per month. Although he did spend a few hundred dollars to fix up his new headquarters, the money he saved in rent allowed him to turn a profit every year that it was in business after the first two. While building his business in New Jersey, he and his wife gave birth to three children: John Jr., Anne Dudley, and Christopher Winston.

During this time, the family's devotion to their church never faltered. The entire family often attended events and mass at the First Presbyterian Church of Englewood. Templeton became involved with fundraising for the church and soon found himself involved with the national activities of the Presbyterian community. In 1940 he was elected to the Commission on Ecumenical Mission and Relations of the National Presbyterian Church and soon was in charge of managing their $50 million investment portfolio.

Juggling his family, community responsibilities, and burgeoning investment business, Templeton was extremely busy. His family had already accumulated a portfolio of around $150,000 in personal assets and with the extra money in hand, Templeton and Dudley decided to take a vacation. Years earlier, while living in Texas, they had taken a trip to the Bahamas that they enjoyed immensely. After discussing their options, they decided that another adventure would be the best way to relax, so in February of 1951, they set off for Bermuda. Unfortunately, while touring the Bermuda countryside on motorbikes, Dudley was severely injured in an accident and was rushed to a hospital, where she succumbed to her injuries.

Templeton and his three children were devastated by the sudden loss of Dudley. He and his family relied heavily on their spiritual resources. In order to further envelop himself in a protective social shield, he took a position on the board of trustees of Princeton Theological Seminary.

Although Templeton took time off of work when he returned from Bermuda, he quickly returned to his company work. Over the next several years, he would make several gestures designed to help his children cope with the loss of their mother, including buying a summer home for his children located on the sound of Long Island in New York. Although he had to work most of the summer weeks, he flew out on weekends keep his children company.

## LOOKING TO THE FUTURE, AND THE TEMPLETON GROWTH FUND

In 1954, Templeton launched a mutual fund, as part of his investment advisory business, known as the Templeton Growth Fund, a first real step in the direction of his soon to be global fame. From the beginning, Templeton believed his competitive advantage was his understanding of global financial markets and, more importantly, how these markets are driven by the characteristics of different people living in various countries. For instance, Templeton had faith in the work ethic of the Japanese. However, World War II wiped out a lot of Japanese infrastructure and impaired the country's ability to regain a foothold on its economy. Templeton knew that although the economy was in shambles, Japanese workers represented a long-term asset and would eventually be able to leverage their strong work ethic in order to return big dividends for his fund (see Figure 4.2).

The mutual fund format Templeton chose was the perfect fit for his fund. Unlike hedge funds, mutual funds are designed around the needs of the common man. They offer everyday investors the opportunity to take

**FIGURE 4.2**   Return of Templeton Growth Fund
*Source:* Historical data from Yahoo! Finance

advantage of profit opportunities normally reserved for wealthy investors and large corporations.

## Templeton's Second Marriage and Fund

In 1958, Templeton remarried Irene Reynolds Butler. He had been running the Templeton Growth Fund for four years and was growing tired of the Northeast. A year later, he sold his investment advisory business to an insurance company and began the process of finding a new base to operate out of. In 1968, Templeton finally settled on where he would make his permanent home: Lyford Cay in the Bahamas.

Between selling his advisory business in 1959 and moving to the Bahamas in 1968, Templeton had a number of important business deals that shaped his life. He had been running his Growth Fund since 1954 and the returns were amazing. In 1956, he partnered with William Damroth to launch the Nucleonics, Chemistry, and Electronics Fund, a specialty fund reflecting his lifelong interest in science and technology.

In the late 1950s specialty funds were popular, especially since the space race was in full swing in the United States. The fund grew dramatically, and in 1962 Templeton sold his stake. Over the next three decades he went on to create some of the most successful international investment funds in history.

By 1974, The Templeton Growth Fund had reached $13 million in assets under management. Despite his success, Templeton was still a relatively unknown name in fund management. Additionally, the mutual fund world had slumped along with the rest of the economy, and Templeton was struggling to grow. John Galbraith came aboard to help the Templeton Growth Fund soar to the next level. Galbraith had a keen ability to connect with the public, and his marketing techniques helped Templeton's Growth Fund reach $100 million under management within just four years.

Galbraith had given Templeton a legendary pitch before he was hired. He claimed that the slow growth of Templeton's Growth Fund was a direct result of poor marketing. Templeton was never an expert on how to market himself and had always relied on word of mouth to help his fund. Galbraith promised that if Templeton brought him on to oversee a new marketing push, he would grow the fund by tenfold in 10 years. This was at a time when, despite its extraordinary performance, the Growth Fund had only grown from $7 million to $13 million during its first 20 years in operation.

Templeton reluctantly agreed, but he knew that Galbraith's skills would fill a serious hole in the management of his company. After a few years of Galbraith's consultation, Templeton launched a second fund, the Templeton World Fund. (Throughout the years, he would also launch several other funds that were focused on certain industries and countries.)

By the time he and Galbraith had launched the World Fund, Templeton's investment workload was too much for him to handle on his own. He hired Tom Hansberger to work out of a Florida office and, several years later, he also hired Mark Holowesko, who eventually became chief investment officer.

## The Bahamas

Upon moving to the Bahamas, Templeton renewed his religious life. The people of the Bahamas have a tradition of religious devotion, unlike many of the people in the United States did at the time, so Templeton felt more at home and founded the Templeton Theological Seminary, the first theological college in the Bahamas.

In order to fully integrate into the Bahamas, which is a British colony, Templeton became a British citizen soon after completing his custom-built home. Despite his beautiful new property, Templeton would still demonstrate the thriftiness that had made him famous. His first office there was composed of two small rooms above a barbershop. Although he had sold most of his business to the insurance firm back in New York, he still retained control of his famed Templeton Growth Fund. He was a thousand miles from Wall Street, but he maintained the phenomenal performance of his fund. Overall, the Bahamas helped give Templeton a unique perspective that he used in his financial analysis.

Later on, in 1992, with Galbraith's promise fulfilled, Galbraith and Templeton merged to form Templeton, Galbraith & Hansberger. Shortly thereafter, with $22 billion in assets under management, the company was sold to Franklin Resources for a reported $913 million. This acquisition made Franklin Resources one of the largest financial conglomerates in the world. By 1997, the fund had four million investors with $80 billion under management. He died in 2008.

## RECREATING TEMPLETON'S TRADING STRATEGIES

A key principle of Templeton's trading strategy was finding the point of greatest pessimism. An inflection point like this is characterized by investors who have become so bleak that they are unwilling to buy even the most fundamentally strong stocks. This was the case at the beginning of World War II when Templeton bought as many underpriced securities as possible.

Figure 4.3 shows a scenario similar to Templeton's famous trade. The bold line represents the composite index of the four underlying stocks, which have been seriously impacted by a market event (in this case, the

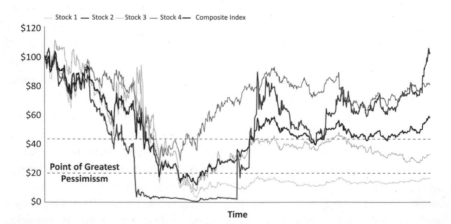

**FIGURE 4.3** Point of Greatest Pessimism
*Source:* Historical data from Yahoo! Finance

recent mortgage crisis). Fearful of the worst, traders entered into a massive selloff, causing prices to dip below their fundamental values. As the composite index dropped below the threshold of pessimism, Templeton would know it was time to buy. With a position in hand, Templeton would wait for the market to realize its mistake and correct itself. With this strategy, the underlying stocks would not perform equally well. For instance, Stock 2 crashes shortly after passing the threshold. Many traders would see this as an indicator that the stock is crashing to zero. Although Stock 2 is the worst performer for a great while, by the end of the holding period, it would have risen above all of the others.

Templeton corrected for this volatility by using only composite indices (such as the bold line), which better represent the market ethos as a whole, to determine where the range of greatest pessimism lies. Even though some of the underlying stocks would shoot up and others would remain cheap, the overall portfolio would increase. In this example, the portfolio of stocks more than doubled in less than a year after it entered the point of greatest pessimism.

## TEMPLETON'S TOP TRAITS

Templeton had an extremely well-rounded and dynamic career as one of the world's foremost expert mutual fund managers. He created value from his knowledge of the international markets while keeping an eye on the morality of what he was doing. He positively affected the lives of millions of people through both his financial advice as well as his religious pursuits. In order to achieve his goals, he maintained a set of core traits that drove his approach to the markets:

- *Thriftiness:* Templeton was proud of his thrift and his ability to make something out of nothing.
- *Common sense:* Templeton's levelheadedness, even in the face of a tumultuous marketplace, was his strength. When the brightest and best-prepared investors lost ground or got emotionally attached to their trades, Templeton knew the best thing for his investors was to keep an even keel and continue with a long-term strategy.
- *Zeal:* Templeton had a zealous approach to his trades. Without exception, all of the managers in this book have a fantastic level of intensity when it comes to trading, but in many ways Templeton took it to the next level. The righteousness of his religious beliefs extended into his

work in the sense that he was working for the good of the world. Becoming a multibillionaire was simply a pleasant side-effect of his good work.

- *Commitment to fundamental analysis:* Templeton was a classic mutual fund manager. He wholeheartedly rejected technical analysis, which became popular with chartists in the 1980s. Instead, he believed that companies' financial forecasts and other fundamental metrics should be scrutinized to project how their performance would affect stock prices over the next several years.

■ ■ ■

All in all, Templeton created a reliable strategy that has been mimicked by many money managers. Templeton's techniques and approach will live on long after his fund.

Next, you will learn the story of Jesse Livermore.

## CHAPTER 5

# Jesse Livermore

## *Legendary Speculator*

Any investor or trader today instantly recognizes the name Jesse Livermore, one of the greatest traders to ever live. Even 70 years after his tragic death, his trading style and opinions on the markets live on.

Livermore traded through two major stock market crashes (1907 and 1929) and profited frequently throughout his career as a trader while enjoying a somewhat lavish lifestyle. He also happened to take great losses often. Both of these things added to his discipline in becoming a better trader.

## LIVERMORE'S HISTORY

Born in the small town of Shrewsbury, Massachusetts, in July 1877, Jesse Livermore grew up poor on his father's farm. From an early age, as is usually common with those growing up on a farm, he worked long hours and did hard, physical labor. He was frail, and work was not easy for him as a child.

Livermore was said to not have enjoyed his childhood and was better with numbers than he was with physical labor. In 1891, with the blessing of his mother, he set out for Boston at the age of 15 and found a job at a Paine Webber office. He began work posting quotes on the "big board" where quotes were gathered.

The stock market that we know today was a lot different back in the late 1890s. Telephones had only recently been invented and were not widely used across the country. Telegraph wires remained a dominating force for the financial industry as stock quotes were tapped across the country. Another important part of the industry was ticker tape. (The phrase "ticker-tape parade" originated when discarded paper tape was thrown out of windows during parades.) Traders would say one could "feel the tape" and get an idea of how a market or particular security was about to move.

There was no high-frequency trading, no electronic exchanges, no dark pools, no esoteric securities—this was trading in its purest form. A popular destination for speculators back in the day was the bucket shop. A bucket shop was an interesting concept because it operated much like a casino. You could place bets that the price of a particular stock would go up or down, but you couldn't actually buy the stock. You merely speculated on a change in price and if your bet was correct, you'd win money. Owners would come up with all sorts of ways to keep their customers from making money, too, including instructing legitimate brokers at the exchanges to move the price of a stock with a large order.

It was the bucket shops of the early 20th century that essentially "taught" Livermore how to trade. He would frequently visit a shop and use his stock market theories to speculate on railroads and other companies. More often than not, Livermore would win and bucket shop owners wouldn't allow him to place bets. Word spread quickly about Livermore's reputation, and soon bucket shops across the country had banned him from making trades. He had a habit of following specific stocks and recording their movements in a small notebook. He would sometimes break out the book before trading and compare it with current market prices. If the trade looked good and correlated with his notes, he'd place a bet.

Livermore soon became known around the shops as The Boy Plunger. In the book *Reminisces of a Stock Operator, Annotated Edition*, it is noted that the nickname came from a combination of Livermore's boyish looks and the term *plunger*, which was reserved for those who risked large sums of capital on moves in the market.

As Livermore traveled the country, he grew tired of not being an actual market participant and of his semipermanent ban from the bucket shops. And so, at the age of 21, he set out for New York City in hopes of making it to the big leagues.

## AT HOME IN NEW YORK

Livermore truly loved finance. His love for the tape, price movements, and the aura of the New York Stock Exchange made him feel right at home in New York. His transition from Boston marked a change in the way he traded; actually having to purchase stocks through a broker and dealing in the markets was a very different game than the one he played in the bucket shops.

But no stock was safe from The Boy Plunger. Livermore traded in everything from railroad companies like Burlington-Northern to U.S. Steel to commodities including sugar and cotton. Because electronic trading didn't exist, by the time you put your order in through your broker and it was transferred to the exchange floor, prices could have moved several points.

Livermore's first brokerage was E.F. Hutton & Co., then known as Harris, Hutton and Company. After losing his initial grubstake (funds advanced to someone in return for a share of the profits), Livermore asked Hutton himself for $500 to do some trading, which he was given. He went out and built up another bundle of money to trade with by perusing bucket shops across the midwestern United States.

Using market sentiment in general was one of the many ways Livermore made successful trades. If it was a bull market, Livermore would buy stocks and ride them up to profits. If it was a bear market, he would sell short stock. Despite having his account blown up in 1901, Livermore recovered and was moderately successful. He began living a very comfortable life and traveled more often—something that he would continue to do whenever he felt the markets were out of sync with his trading methods. While a successful trader, Livermore had a habit of frequently losing his winnings. It was a recurring situation that left him troubled due to his taste for the finer things.

No one knows exactly when, but at some point, Livermore realized he needed to evolve his trading methods in order to adapt to ever-changing markets.

### Fame and Fortune

Livermore was a speculator, and he used a proprietary system to conduct what he thought were money-winning trades. Speculation, of course, is a fancy way of gambling, and many people simply think they have some kind of edge that gives them a surefire way to win. Throughout Livermore's career, he would frequently get tips from other traders and brokerages that seemed too good to be true. Usually, they were, and Livermore would engage in a heavy loss that would put him back in a place where he'd have little money and need to build up his stake once again.

Back in the day, brokerage offices and bucket shops were all over the place: boardwalks, hotels, and other high-traffic areas. One meeting in a hotel lobby, according to Lefèvre's *Reminiscences*, details a point at which Livermore became interested in commodity markets and not just stocks after looking for a brokerage house with better execution. It was said he liked commodity markets because they were less prone to manipulation. Cotton would be the subject of one of Livermore's worst trades ever. Following his spectacular win by shorting stocks in the stock market crash of 1907, he tried to corner the cotton market and instead it left him broke.

Always refining his trading style, Livermore even worked with technical analysis, buying stocks when they were breaking out and moving higher and shorting them when they broke downward. He would also use the news to his advantage. While Livermore never tried to outright predict the news, he would plan his trades along the path of least resistance. For example, when fighting broke out between Germany and Britain, during World War I in 1915, Livermore was short the market and used the opportunity to cover his shorts for a profit.

## The Panic of 1907

The 1907 stock market crash was Livermore's first big trading opportunity. In 1907, America was in the midst of a recession. Throughout the year, commodity prices were volatile amid increased speculation from investors. A man named F. Augustus Heinze, who owned the United Copper Company, had a brother who tried unsuccessfully to corner the company's stock. He began buying en masse with the help of Charles Barney, president of the Knickerbocker Trust Company. What happened is as follows:

> *On Monday, October 14, he began aggressively purchasing shares of United Copper, which rose in one day from $39 to $52 per share. On Tuesday, he issued the call for short sellers to return the borrowed stock. The share price rose to nearly $60, but the short sellers were able to find plenty of United Copper shares from sources other than the Heinzes.*[1]

The price of United Copper began to collapse, and along with it shares on the New York Stock Exchange market began to tumble. Runs on banks began throughout New York City and elsewhere, adding to the panic. The events were so bad that famous financier John Pierpont Morgan (yes, that J. P. Morgan) had to step in with heads of banks and trust companies in order to guarantee depositor withdraws. A similar occurrence happened at the New York Stock Exchange as it began to crash on October 24, 1907. Morgan brought a group of bank presidents together to pledge over $23 million to keep the exchange from breaking down completely.

Livermore spotted the trouble early on and shorted stocks all the way down the NYSE. By the time he covered, he had made over $3 million in a six-week period. It's said that he was able to spot the lack of capital from market participants required to buy stocks and that this would mean short sellers could easily drive down prices. While never confirmed, the events certainly seem to correlate rather well.

The event granted Livermore wealth beyond his dreams, but trouble followed soon. Livermore became engaged in speculating on corn and wheat contracts in Chicago and soon considered himself very savvy. He began trading heavily in cotton and had moderate success, but it was soon short-lived. Livermore engaged in a trade in which he increasingly built up a large position in cotton and was ultimately crushed when a series of unfortunate events switched the bullish nature of the market to the downside as he kept buying in an attempt to keep the price from dropping any further.

This violated one of Livermore's key beliefs: never add to a losing position in an attempt to sway the market because you will get blown out. The event nearly erased the entire $3 million stake Livermore had earned in the crash of 1907. He soon recovered, though, clearing nearly half a million dollars on a trade involving Union Pacific stock.

## The Crash of 1929

Livermore used the panic of 1907 as a learning experience when he hit a winning streak during the 1920s. An excellent bull market was in place (similar, by the way, to that of the mid-1980s), and Livermore was riding it to the top. As you can see in Figure 5.1, the runup to each respective crash can be seen in this historical data. (Any of these crashes are similar in fashion and could be used as a barometer.)

Having been through the panic in 1907, Livermore began to recognize the market conditions in 1929 as eerily similar to those of 1907. He shorted

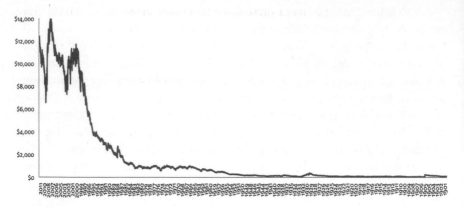

**FIGURE 5.1**  Historical Chart of the Dow Jones Industrial Index from the early 1900s to present

various stocks on the New York Stock Exchange as the market began to collapse.

The crash of 1929 was due to a speculative bubble, similar to that of 1907. But the 1929 crash—the worst crash in the history of the markets—would be much more devastating to both the markets and economy as a whole. When all was said and done, though, Livermore not only survived the ordeal (unlike many other Americans and investors), but he also was $100 million richer.

## LIVERMORE'S TRAGIC END

Little information is known about Livermore's life over the 10 years before his death in 1940. A lot of situations throughout Livermore's life were tragic and grim. For instance, he married his first wife, Nettie Jordan, in 1900. During a dispute over an event in which Livermore had lost everything, he begged Nettie to pawn some of her jewelry. She refused, and the couple ended up divorcing in 1917. A year later, Livermore married his second wife, Dorothy Wendt. An excerpt from the December 18, 1918, issue of the *Lake Placid News* details the event:

> *Miss Dorothy Wendt and Jesse Livermore were married recently. Both are known here, Mr. Livermore having purchased High Knolls on Signal hill for his fiancée last year. The groom known in Wall Street as the "boy plunger" married Miss Wendt the day after his divorce from the former Nettie Jordan.*[2]

Jesse and Dorothy went on to have two sons: Jesse Jr. and Paul Livermore. Jesse Jr. committed suicide in 1976 and Jesse Jr.'s son, Jesse III, did the same in 2006.

After his marriage to Wendt failed, Livermore married Harriet Metz Noble in 1933. Shortly afterward, through a series of losses, Livermore found himself broke once again and was suspended in 1934 from the Chicago Board of Trade. No doubt, being banned must have made Livermore even more depressed after being wiped out financially because he ended up committing suicide at the Sherry Netherland hotel on Fifth Avenue in New York City in 1940[3]. Again, the Lake Placid News discusses the tragedy of his death:

> *A radio news flash last night reported that Jesse Livermore, 62, committed suicide yesterday in New York City. Livermore was once known in financial circles as the "boy wonder" of Wall Street, where he made a fortune while still a comparatively young man.*[4]

Before committing suicide, he was encouraged by his sons to write a book on trading. The result was *How to Trade in Stocks*, published by Duell, Sloan and Pearce in March 1940. It went over Livermore's trading ideologies one by one on everything from technical analysis to things such as anticipating the current direction of the market.

If you are interested in reading a staple in investing literature about Jesse Livermore and his importance as an historical figure in finance, pick up a copy of the book *Reminiscences of a Stock Operator* by journalist Edwin Lefèvre. First published in 1923, a semifictional account of a trader named "Larry Livingston," the book is relatively in line with Livermore's actual travels and trades and for the most part is accurate. Rumor has it that Livermore and Lefèvre actually worked together on the book in the 1920s, but this has yet to be confirmed.

Most people think it is one of the greatest books ever written on the subject of trading. I also highly recommend picking up the 2009 *Annotated Edition* of *Reminiscences of a Stock Operator*, which features incredibly informative notation from Jon Markman, an MSN Money columnist and an award-winning journalist, popular market analyst, and veteran fund manager in his own right. (Full disclosure: The *Annotated Edition* is published by John Wiley & Sons, which is also the publisher of this book.)

The *Annotated Edition* blurs the line between the truth and fiction in the novel. Plus, it's incredibly historic and gives you insight into how things worked so many years ago in relatively different times.

## AN EXAMPLE OF LIVERMORE'S INFLUENCE TODAY

As mentioned throughout this chapter, Jesse Livermore was an incredibly influential trader and continues to influence traders. In an interview with my friend, Joshua Brown of Fusion Analytics (and author of the web site *The Reformed Broker* at www.thereformedbroker.com), we discussed how Livermore influences his investment styles and disciplines:

**Vince:**    Why do you think Jesse Livermore is still so famous among the trading community even 70 years after his death?

**Joshua:**   The quasi-autobiography of Livermore (*Reminiscences of a Stock Operator*) set forth a number of unwritten rules of trading that are as practicable and essential now as they were in the early 20th century. His discussions about tipsters, respecting trends, recognizing market characteristics, and position sizing are still the gospel. Every serious trader can recite whole passages of the book on demand.

**Vince:**    Do you think that his ability to navigate not one but two stock market crashes was unprecedented?

**Joshua:**   I'm sure there were traders who had done it, but probably not with the same panache. And how many of them had biographers?

**Vince:**    Livermore won big in those two crashes, but several times over he nearly lost (or did lose) it all. What do you think were some of his flaws? Do you think he lacked self-discipline?

**Joshua:**   Livermore happened to have excelled at a skill that ultimately made him rich but kept him constantly on edge. After a lifetime of panic and anxiety, he ultimately took his own life in 1940, the same year that his book came out. I think there is a cautionary tale in Jesse's life about handling the ups and downs of the market on an emotional basis, not just a financial one.

**Vince:**    What can traders today learn by studying Jesse Livermore's techniques and views on the markets?

**Joshua:**   Traders can take a very valuable lesson away just by considering how influential the book is decades after its first publication. That lesson is that there are rules to this game; (there are) certain disciplines that have always been true and should not be violated.

. . .

When a trader breaks his core ideology, it's the beginning of the end. Traders need to obey their disciplines to remain good whether they win or lose individual trades.

## RECREATING LIVERMORE'S TRADING STRATEGIES

Livermore was invested in the market at an unprecedented time. Turmoil was in full swing during both the 1907 and 1929 crashes, and even the financial crisis of 2007–2009 doesn't fully compare. One could argue that by shorting financials during the 2007–2009 crisis and then buying them back in early 2009, a trader was making a trade similar to Livermore's legendary moves, but the stock market was a very different place when Livermore was trading it and we'll just never have exactly similar markets thanks to the advent of electronic trading. However, for the sake of getting into the mind-set of recreating some of Livermore's trading strategies, we can talk about indices. The S&P 500, the most popular U.S. stock market index, is perfect for trading. There's an ETF of it, called SPDR S&P 500 ETF, which is offered by State Street.

A way to make profits off daily market swings involves the S&P 500 E-Mini contract traded at CME Group. Looking at Figure 5.2, you can see that the E-Mini contract looks just like the S&P 500's performance. These contracts (ES), are highly liquid and are traded outside of equity market hours (normal hours are 9:30 A.M. to 4:00 P.M. EST). They give traders the ability to make speculative trades like the ones Livermore made.

## LIVERMORE'S TOP TRAITS

Livermore perfected his use of reading the tape, and he also stuck to a few key principles throughout most of his career. He got into trouble or lost money when he broke these three principles:

1. *Remain confident:* Livermore was a speculator through and through and had a method for how to trade in both bull and bear markets. He has been quoted as saying, "You cannot fight the tape." If you invest

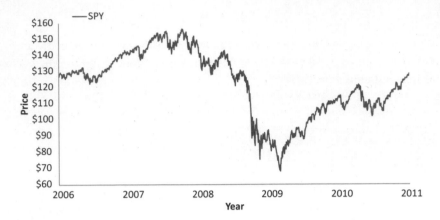

**FIGURE 5.2**  Past performance of the S&P 500
*Source:* Historical data from Yahoo! Finance

with diligence, you will succeed. It's not to say that there aren't short-ing opportunities in a market, but rather that you can take your profits higher by riding the coattails of a general trend.

2. *Go with the flow:* If you are clearly in a bear market, then it's probably a good idea to partake in some short selling and not bet on short-term growth from stocks. The same goes for a bull market: don't fight the trend. At the moment, we are in the midst of a bullish trend driven by the Federal Reserve's policy of quantitative easing. Do not fight the Fed. The smart thing to do is to go long and lock in your gains when you begin to sense a pullback or correction. You can always get back in again if it goes higher.

3. *Don't average losers:* Lots of traders will agree with this one. When in a losing position, bite the bullet and cut your losses. It's worse to double up on a losing position in the hope that a trend will reverse. This point is chronicled in some of the most popular investing literature out there. Jack Schwager's *Market Wizards* and Marty Schwartz's *Pitbull* both write that when traders double down on a losing trade it can be a horrible idea. It's exactly what happened to Livermore with cotton, and he admitted it. This logic can also be applied outside of trading, as with card games and other forms of gambling. Although it isn't everything, there is a lot of luck in trading. It takes finesse, skill, and experience to become a top trader like Livermore.

■ ■ ■

Remember that one key downfall of Livermore's career was that he speculated on the market using advice given to him by others. When someone gives you a hot tip for a trade, chances are it's too late to profit from it.

To use Livermore's experience to avoid some of the mistakes he made, you need to believe in yourself and stick to your guns. Don't let outside forces trick you into thinking there are foolproof ways to win at trading, because all it takes is someone with more capital, better tools, and better skills to slap you like a hockey puck.

Next up, we'll take a look at the trading style of John Paulson.

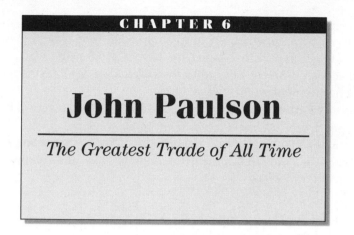

## CHAPTER 6

# John Paulson

## *The Greatest Trade of All Time*

J ohn Paulson was relatively unknown to the retail investing public up until the financial crisis of 2007–2009. Paulson's upbringing and background was pretty average and not your typical "stuff of legends." Born in 1955 in Queens, New York, he attended Public Schools 193 and 194 and Bayside High School, participating in the gifted-class programs. After graduating from high school, he attended one of the top business schools in the world of finance, New York University's College of Business and Public Administration (now known as Stern Business School).

After finishing his undergraduate degree at NYU, Paulson earned his MBA from Harvard Business School, where he was designated a Baker Scholar for graduating in the top 5 percent of his class. It was time for Paulson to begin climbing the corporate ladder. Paulson went on to become the largest merger arbitrage specialist and major player in many M&A and event-driven transactions. Little did anyone know that nearly 25 years after beginning his career, John Paulson would become one of the richest men in the world because of one trade.

## PAULSON'S EARLY CAREER

Paulson earned his chops by beginning work as a management consultant at Boston Consulting Group, the firm behind the famous "growth-share matrix," which helps companies identify how to best allocate cash within their business.

He spent 1980 to 1982 at Boston Consulting Group before moving to Odyssey Partners, a smart, sophisticated hedge fund that was making a name for itself (in part, thanks to Leon Levy, a gentleman today known for several accomplishments, including the cofounding of Oppenheimer & Co. and the proliferation of the mutual fund).

Odyssey Partners proved to be a solid place for Paulson to gain footing in the practice of investing. Subsequently he went on to be a managing director in the merger arbitrage department of Bear Stearns and a Partner at Gruss & Co., which both served as foundations (and funding) for his hedge fund: Paulson & Co.

## Paulson & Co.

Paulson & Co., Inc. began in 1994 with $2 million of capital from Paulson and a few other investors. Starting with only two employees (Paulson and his secretary), Paulson knew he had to build a track record before reaching his goal of attracting outside investors.

And investors he got. In the 1990s, the economic sentiment was one of growth. Alan Greenspan was the chairman of the Federal Reserve, and dot-com companies and technology were slowly building into a bubble as economic growth was increasing at a steady pace. In other words, it was a lovely time for Paulson to have a hedge fund in which he could court investors for money while increasing the amount of assets under management. The Dow Jones Industrial Average—the weighted index that every investor in America was glued to—shot up like a rocketship, going from a little under 4,000 in the mid-1990s to nearly 12,000 in late 2007. You could basically throw darts at stock tickers written on a piece of paper and anywhere they landed, you'd enjoy returns.

## THE GREATEST TRADE

Paulson's experience in merger arbitrage and event-driven investing would be a key component of his bet against subprime mortgages. Starting in 2005, Paulson saw that the U.S. housing market was turning and could not sustain itself at the rate of growth it had enjoyed for years. With hindsight on our side, it's something most of us can now easily see.

There are solid reasons why the housing crisis happened, and one of them was the home equity line of credit (HELOC). A HELOC, one of the most interesting schemes of recent years, works like this: Say you have a house worth $100,000 in 2000. As 2002 rolls around, an appraiser comes by and, sure enough, with the housing market exploding all over the country, your home has significantly increased in value. It is now worth $150,000 and you are as happy as can be. With your home worth more than the original purchase price, you might want to sell if you were a speculator on real estate, but you don't want to sell it because you live in it. You *have* been eyeing a new boat for some time, though, and would like to purchase it and pay it off in installments. This is where the HELOC comes in. The HELOC allows you to go to a bank and draw out the extra equity from your home as a line of credit—in our boat example, let's say you take $50,000 over time, similar to a mortgage. You use that line of credit in the form of a credit card or another financial instrument to go buy whatever you please, or maybe you refinance your existing mortgage. The first 5 to 10 years could consist of *interest-only* payments and then the following 15 to 20 would pay down principal. But, as with most things in life, there is a caveat. In this instance, there are several.

Unlike a mortgage, in which the interest rate is calculated on a 12-month year, a HELOC's interest payment is calculated daily. A month with 31 days as opposed to 30 means that you will be paying more for that month as opposed to a mortgage. This becomes very risky due to the fact that a change in the prime lending rate will increase or decrease your payments without notice.

One issue is that your home is now acting as the collateral for this line of credit. You buy that boat and maybe don't even realize until later that you can't afford the payments on your HELOC. The bank can then come and take your house and sell it and you're stuck with whatever is left over after the bank is done. Sure, you may have close to $100,000 or something like that, but now you're homeless! Another issue is the home equity itself. If the real estate market begins to falter and the value of your home declines, then you're automatically in trouble. Your lender can cut off your line of credit at a moment's notice because it now knows that the collateral is worth less than the loan.

And so, in late 2005, when Deutsche Bank securitization whiz Greg Lippmann began cooking up credit default swaps on mortgage-backed securities and selling them to the few smarter/luckier/more creative banks like Goldman Sachs, Paulson also wanted to buy some. In a July 2007 interview with *Pensions & Investments* magazine, Paulson explains the beauty of securitization and how easy it is to take a position on the products.

> *The beauty of shorting a bond is that the maximum you can lose*
> *is the spread over the benchmark; yet if the bond defaults, you*
> *can potentially make more. So it's an asymmetrical risk-return*

*tradeoff. In the case of subprime securities, we targeted the triple-B bonds, which are the lowest tranches in the subprime securitization.*

*In a typical securitization, you have 18 to 20 different tranches with the lowest. . . . taking the first loss. The triple-B bond has about 5% subordination, meaning that if the loss is greater than 5%, the bond will be impaired. And if it's more than 6%, the bond will be extinguished. The yield was only 1% over LIBOR (the London interbank offered rate) so by shorting this particular bond, if I was wrong, I could lose 1%, but if I was right, I could make 100%. The downside was very limited but it had very substantial upside, and we like those types of investments.*[1]

Paulson took on little risk in hopes of a big reward, and that's what he got. After buying up credit default swaps on the worst of the worst mortgage bonds and securities, Paulson waited. The newly created swaps had a very small market, and the impact of the collapse of the housing market was not yet in full swing. But that was okay because Paulson knew his investment would not be a quick payday. It would take time and patience for his bets to pay off. When they paid off, though, they did so handsomely: At the end of 2007, Paulson's investment returned $15 billion for him and his investors, making it one of the largest payouts and greatest trades ever made. The next year he would garner an additional $5 billion for Paulson & Co., making the fleet of institutional investors backing him extremely happy and making him a very, very rich man.

If Paulson had the opportunity to give something of the equivalent of an Oscar speech, he would probably say one of the typical phrases like, "I couldn't have done it alone," because he did have some help in the trade. Paolo Pellegrini, a sharp-minded Italian who had climbed the ranks at Harvard Business School, was Paulson's lieutenant and helped guide him through the derivatives jungles. Pellegrini was completely under the radar and worked at an old investment house, Lazard Freres. Sick of his inability to outperform at the firm, though, he went looking to make a name for himself. In 2005, he called Paulson and asked him if he had a position available. Paulson offered him a role as an analyst at his firm and Pellegrini took it.

Over the next year, the investment strategies that Paulson had crafted at Bear Stearns and Odyssey were put into play with Pellegrini acting as support. While not entirely an expert in certain subjects, Pellegrini's ability to understand complex financial structures and derivatives language was key to his work with Paulson. He pored over troves of government data and put pieces together that would lend information on America's housing market running amok. Together Pellegrini and Paulson placed their bet that it was going to crash, and held their breath collectively.

After Paulson & Co. made its billions on the bet, Pellegrini reaped his share of the pot and took his millions to launch his own hedge fund, PSQR Capital. Of course, before launching the new fund, it was reported he bought a Ferrari and a nice New York Upper West Side apartment to celebrate his riches. Just a few years later, though, in August 2010, Pellegrini shocked the investment world by closing PSQR to outside investors despite stellar returns of 61 percent in 2009. Simply put, Pellegrini was not content with market conditions and decided to focus on preserving wealth rather than simply speculating on generating alpha for investors.

■ ■ ■

If we return to 2007/2008, we can go into detail about when Paulson placed his bet on American foreclosures ramping up. Some people have argued that Paulson's bet against American homeowners was immoral because he made money on the misfortunes of others, but it can be viewed in a different light: His bet actually showcases his ability to make an unbiased, unaffected investment decision. Paulson was simply making a bet as a trader that he believed was absolute and correct.

The housing market reached its peak by 2007 and the stock market—driven by the housing market through the 2000s, similar to how it had been driven by the dot-com bubble in the late 1990s—had also hit its apex. Paulson had his bets placed via various derivatives contracts that were packaged full of collateralized debt obligations (CDOs) backed by lousy mortgages, like the ABACUS deal. ABACUS became a hot topic during 2010 when the Securities and Exchange Commission sued Goldman Sachs for packaging together CDOs. Common to the synthetic CDO collateral process, Paulson had input but the final authority and selection process lay with ACA Capital, a monoline bond insurance company who went long the CDOs.

Paulson took the short side of the trade, and Goldman Sachs, acting as a market maker, pawned off the long side of the trade to investment houses such as ABN Amro. Ultimately, Goldman settled the case out of court. Paulson was not accused of any wrongdoing and was not a party to the SEC lawsuit. But by using these carefully crafted securitizations,

Paulson saw his bets pay off in full. He earned $3.7 billion in total compensation in 2007, according to *Portfolio* magazine:[2]

> *Paulson & Co.'s funds (with an estimated $36 billion under management and growing by the day) were up a staggering $15 billion as the markets teetered in 2007; one fund gained 590 percent, another 353 percent. All this reportedly garnered him a personal payday of $3.7 billion, among the biggest in history.*

It was an unprecedented bet that in turn paid an unprecedented amount of money. Paulson was at the top of his game, and his future as one of the world's shrewdest investors was set in stone. From there, 2008 continued to pay off for Paulson & Co.—albeit not as much as 2007 did—and in 2009, he began planning his next strategy after successfully navigating the 2007–2008 crisis.

■ ■ ■

Recovery was on everyone's mind in 2009. In 2008, the Standard & Poor's 500 Index had declined by a staggering 38.49 percent. The stock market rallied into 2009 and beyond, gaining 23.5 percent for 2009. But stocks weren't the only thing rallying. The financial crisis had scared investors with mutual funds and other investments, many of which were in process of being wiped out. Gold was soaring and investors both domestic and abroad headed to the time-tested precious metal. In the fall of 2008, gold was trading at around $700 per troy ounce. By late 2009, the price of gold was well above $1,000 and was headed to the stars. It has since engaged in a pullback/correction of sorts, but why this obsession with gold prices, you might ask? Because Paulson bet big on gold after he collected on the housing market bet.

Since mid-2009 (and possibly before then), Paulson began to invest in physical gold, gold exchange-traded funds, and stocks of gold-mining companies. He is one of the largest owners (if not the largest owner) of shares of the SPDR gold ETF offered by State Street Global Advisors, and he has a substantial amount of shares in the following companies: AngloGold Ashanti Ltd., Kinross Gold Corp., and Gold Fields Ltd. According to StreetInsider.com, Paulson sees gold going to $2,400 to $4,000 an ounce by 2012. Should that happen, his direct investments in gold alone would more than double and his equity holdings would also increase by a substantial amount.

Another investment Paulson is currently big on, ironically, involves betting on homebuilders and a recovery in the U.S. housing market. This bet will take some time to pay off, though, as the economy and the housing market take more time than thought to recover. CNBC's Maneet Ahuja summarized the bet nicely:

> *Paulson, who manages the $31 billion Paulson & Co. fund, has made a "stalking horse" bid of $42.4 million to acquire the assets of Engle Homes, which includes land and lots in Arizona targeted for more than 8,000 homes, and nine completed residences.*[3]

The current economic landscape in America today is unpredictable, though. The latest data from Case-Shiller/Standard & Poor's shows that home price increases have decelerated of late (at the time of this writing, at least). Ben Bernanke and the Federal Reserve continue to implement rounds of quantitative easing by printing money in the hopes that the economy will continue to grow and housing will recover.

Over the coming years, quantitative easing will also play a role in the recovery of America's banking system, something Paulson had originally bet quite a bit of his fund's money on.

However, as of early November 2010, a 13-F filing with the SEC showed he had sold off some of his equity in banks like Citigroup and Bank of America, although he still holds large stakes.

## RECREATING PAULSON'S TRADING STRATEGIES

Paulson's housing short during the recent financial crisis appears similar to the trades involving Kyle Bass we discussed in Chapter 1. In the case of Paulson, he used a variety of complex derivatives to take huge profits on the collapse of the U.S. housing market. As I've mentioned, you could use CME housing futures or the SPDR S&P Homebuilders ETF to put on your trade.

More important, though, is how Paulson has kept generating stellar returns, even postcrisis. His gold play made his investors a fortune when gold prices soared during 2010 (see Figure 6.1). You can see how being long gold was an excellent idea.

There are many ways to play gold. The first is to buy gold outright. You can buy bullion or coins or even jewelry. This is a tad impractical for a

**FIGURE 6.1**  Gold Prices in 2010
*Source:* Historical data from Yahoo! Finance

trader, but could work for a small investor looking for the value of gold to rise over a long period.

The second way is to use an exchange-traded fund. State Street's SPDR Gold Trust ETF (Ticker: GLD) is one of the most popular gold-based ETFs. You buy it, just like a stock, and hope the price of gold goes up. If it does, the value of shares in the ETF increases. See Figure 6.2 for an example of performance of GLD from January of 2009 to January of 2011.

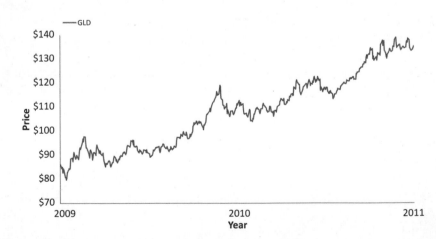

**FIGURE 6.2**  Past performance of SPDR Gold Trust ETF
*Source:* Historical data from Yahoo! Finance

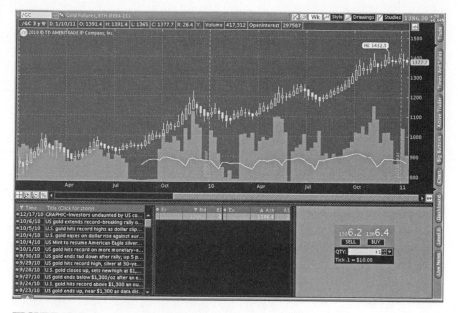

**FIGURE 6.3** CME Group gold contracts
*Source:* Historical data from TD Thinkorswim

The third way you could trade gold involves playing the futures market. You can trade CME Group's gold contracts (GC) or even the new E-mini gold contracts, which are aimed at smaller, retail investors. Future can provide an idea of what traders' current thoughts are on gold. In Figure 6.3, you can see how these contracts performed from 2009 into 2010.

As for playing the banks, you can simply buy options or stock like Bank of America, Morgan Stanley, Goldman Sachs, Citigroup, and other financial institutions and short them if you think we're due for another crisis or go long if you think the recovery is in full gear.

## PAULSON'S TOP TRAITS

Paulson, without a doubt, executed the single greatest trade of all time. Three key traits you can learn from by heeding the lessons put forth by Paulson's trading style are:

1. *Heed Paulson's mantra:* "Take care of the downside and the up- side takes care of itself." The beauty of the subprime trade was its

asymetrical nature. What this means is that the downside was defined and minimal while the upside was limitless—the perfect trade if you will. The trick is first not to lose money and then to compound positive returns over many years.

2. *Always be aware of the contrarian perspective:* A lot of the traders we are discussing in this book take contrarian stances with their trades. Bucking the trend in an obvious bull market or bear market can be hard, but if your hypothesis is correct, the payoff can be enormous.

3. *Remain true to the trading style you're successful at*: Paulson focused on a certain skill set and ran with it. One can argue that merger arbitrage has nothing to do with housing markets, but the underlying principal is the same: identify an opportunity to profit and put your money where your mouth is.

■ ■ ■

Paulson's recent bet cemented his future among greats like Paul Tudor Jones and Jesse Livermore. Chances are he will continue to flourish, no matter the market conditions. His prowess is a testament to intelligent investing.

Next up, George Soros.

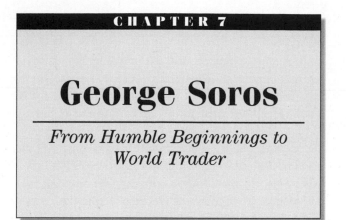

## CHAPTER 7

# George Soros

## *From Humble Beginnings to World Trader*

George Soros is a legend among the hedge fund community. Coming from a humble background, Soros has become one of the most internationally adept traders in the history of the modern financial markets. His life has been chock-full of trials and tribulations, which have molded his business philosophy into a refined machine that has generated countless returns for his investors as well as created him a personal fortune of over $14 billion.

Born in 1930, Soros's life started in Budapest, Hungary, during the tumultuous times of Nazi expansion into Eastern Europe. Coming from a Jewish family, he spent his early years hiding from people wishing to cause him harm.

After the war, Soros headed to England, where he attended the London School of Economics. There he picked up a lifelong passion for philosophy. After a short stint working in northern England, Soros had his first exposure to the financial markets working in the City as a commodities arbitrageur—a job that, he would later admit, he languished at.

When Soros moved to New York, he hit the ground running. As an expert in the European financial markets, he was a hot commodity in the recently protectionist United States. Soros soaked up all he could about working in the financial markets and quickly set off on his own. From there on, he built a reputation as an international trading legend, and the time defined the rest of his illustrious career.

## SOROS'S FAMOUS TRADES

Soros has built a long career around asset management driven by sound research and fundamental analysis. However, his fame has largely come from the few times that he has created dramatic returns for his investors through his ability to predict the movements of the financial fabric holding the international marketplace together.

Soros has always had a unique vision for the financial markets. This was seen early in his career in what would become his first well-known financial predictions. In the 1950s, Germany had seen an incredible real estate boom. Allianz, a well-known German insurance company, had an immense portfolio of real estate that it had acquired after World War II. Despite the appreciation of these assets, the market had not adjusted its valuation of Allianz. In Soros's mind, this meant that the company's shares were selling at a deep discount when compared to its real assets. Soros advised his manager at Wertheim & Co. of his analysis and wrote a paper of advising market participants to buy shares in Allianz. Morgan Guaranty, a manager of the Dreyfus Fund, was immediately interested in the young analyst's work, and almost immediately it began buying up shares of Allianz. The management of Allianz was not pleased and quickly drafted a letter to Soros' boss at Wertheim. By the time is arrived, it was already too late; the shares of Allianz had tripled and Soros won great praise from his superiors.

By the late 1960s, Soros had outgrown his post at Wertheim & Co. and moved to Arnhold & S. Bleichroeder, where he would focus solely on international arbitrage, a job that he was uniquely qualified for. Shortly after joining the new firm, Soros convinced his managers to allow him to set up and manage a pair of offshore funds. The first, called the First Eagle Fund, was a long-only fund. This structure allowed Soros to choose a basket of stocks that he believed to be undervalued by the market and wait for their price to skyrocket. The second fund, known as the Double Eagle Fund, was Soros's first hedge fund. Started with $250,000 of his own money, Soros's fund soon elicited over $6 million from outside investors.

Although much of what Soros did to set up his funds has since become well known, he was a trailblazer for much of the later development in the fund management industry. Although the fund was run from Soros's New York office, it was set up in Curacao in the Dutch Antilles. This allowed investors to escape oversight from the Securities and Exchange Commission (SEC) and capital-gains taxes. In order to maintain the significant tax advantages of his funds, Soros restricted membership to investors who resided primarily outside of the United States.

In 1969, Soros made his first big gain for his new funds. A new investment vehicle known as the real estate investment trust (REIT) was gaining popularity. A REIT is simply a corporation designed to hold and operate real estate for larger entities. A firm operating as a REIT would buy a piece of property, lease it to an external entity, and if the value of the property skyrocketed, sell the property for a profit. The value of the REIT is derived from the cash flow of the holding company as well as the fluctuating value of the underlying real estate. Realizing the cyclical nature of these securities, Soros predicted that there would be an approximate three-year boom-and-bust cycle. Soros traded on this analysis, netting millions in profits for his young fund. His analysis was so accurate that Soros made money on both the upswing of REITs as well as during their decline in 1974.

Soros made a second bet based on the same boom/bust prediction model. In the early days of his fund, a mini tech boom had been developing on Wall Street. High-tech companies had been going on acquisition sprees, funded by the cash provided by private equity companies based on the promise of future earnings that these synergies would one day yield. Noticing the fervor that was developing, Soros bought heavily and timed his exit perfectly. Again, he increased the value of his fund.

Soros continued using his method of predicting boom and busts in the marketplace to help grow his fund by 3,365 percent between 1969 and 1980. Despite the success of this strategy, Soros also had other tools in his financial kit. Building on his early success with Allianz, Soros had an uncanny ability to identify good investments that the rest of Wall Street was unwilling or unable to take advantage of. One such opportunity came about in the early 1970s. Following the Vietnam War, defense contractors had begun to hemorrhage money. After several disappointing years, most Wall Street analysts had written most defense firms off as a lost cause, but Soros was never so sure.

In 1973, Egyptian and Syrian armed forces launched a devastating attack on Israel, destroying entire battalions of American-engineered tanks and airplanes. Although most analysts ignored the financial implications of this development, Soros believed that this signaled that America's military technology was critically antiquated. Warfare had been rapidly evolving, and the next generation of battle gear would invariably integrate a level of technological sophistication that had yet to be seen on the battlefield.

All of this technology would cost a great deal of money. After several meetings with Pentagon officials, Soros and his team became increasingly convinced that defense companies were about to get a huge influx of government contracts. In particular, Soros took note of the specific components that were in need of renewal and sought out investments in the manufacturers that were uniquely positioned to take advantage of an impending increase in demand. He knew that electronic warfare equipment, especially sophisticated aircraft countermeasures, would be critical for the modernization of America's planes. By 1975, Soros and his fund had huge investments in Northrop, United Aircraft, Grumman, and Lockheed. Suddenly, the Pentagon launched the massive revitalization effort that Soros had foreseen, resulting in astronomical earnings for his fund (see Figure 7.1).

Throughout the rest of the 1970s, Soros had a slew of fantastic market predictions. This text, from a *Wall Street Journal* article, describes Soros's market prowess:

> *Over the years the [Soros] has shown a knack for buying stocks before they come into vogue and unloading them at the peak of their popularity. [He] generally ignores stocks widely held by the major mutual funds, bank trust departments and other institutions except as short-sale opportunities.*

In 1979, Soros renamed his fund The Quantum Fund, a reference to the latent uncertainty in quantum mechanics. This was largely a reference and, in part, an admission of Soros's submission to the systemic uncertainty that

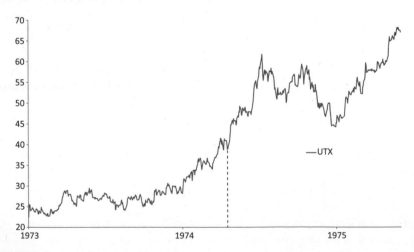

**FIGURE 7.1**  United Aircraft Trade
*Source:* Historical data from Yahoo! Finance

plagues the financial markets. Despite his success, Soros's market prowess was not infallible. During the crash of 1987, the Quantum Fund lost an estimated $650 million to $800 million, most of it in only a few weeks.

All of the dramatic ups and downs of Soros's career had taught him a great deal about managing money in the fluctuating and fickle financial markets. However, up until this point in his career, Soros had purposely kept out of the limelight. He had created large fortunes for his investors. In 1992, Soros made a trade that finally put him on the world stage. For several years, Soros had been following the developments in European currencies. For most of the twentieth century, countries around the world were a part of a de facto fixed exchange rate, first via the gold standard and then via the Bretton Woods agreement. Even as these worldwide systems collapsed, however, many European countries continued to want a consolidated international exchange system.

This system, which at the time was embodied in the European Exchange Rate Mechanism, or ERM, was the precursor to what would become the European Monetary Union. Despite the idealism of this system, Soros knew that the mechanics of getting all of the European central governments to cooperate on international fiscal policy was a tenuous proposition at best. Great Britain, having been the most recent dominant power in Europe, stood at the center of the pending disaster due to the ongoing perception amongst the British parliament that it was still the seat of power in Europe.

This led Soros to predict that the ERM system would inevitably break down, pushing the value of the British pound dramatically down along with many other leading European countries. Soros took on huge leveraged bets against the pound as well as other European currencies. After a long, dramatic battle with the political powers that had vested interests in the success of the pound, the ERM finally collapsed in September 1992, and Soros netted a total of about $2 billion in what was one of the most profitable single trades in the history of the financial markets.

Soros's massive winnings from his bet against Europe won him as much international praise as it did hatred. Soros had effectively made money while an entire region struggled to hold on to its financial system, a scenario that the socialist-leaning London press did not endorse.

## THE HARDSHIPS OF A TRADING GENIUS

The story of George Soros begins on the dreary streets of 1930s Budapest in what is now known as Hungary. The young Soros was witness to dramatic changes to the fundamental fabric of his beloved homeland, and it helped shape much of his political and social world outlooks for the rest of his life.

Soros watched helplessly as a wave of Nazism and Fascism washed over Budapest. Over the previous decade, Hungary had begun to rely on trade with neighboring Germany and Italy in order to claw its way out of a seemingly endless cycle of economic depression. Nazism and Fascism had seeped into the deepest corners of Hungarian politics and had transformed the country into a puppet of the Axis powers of the Second World War.

By 1944, the 14-year-old Soros had watched as most of the Jewish communities were wiped out by invading Nazis. His father, Tivadar, had already seen the German war machine during World War I and had changed their family name from Schwartz to Soros in order to hide their Jewish heritage. Tivadar knew that he would have to blend his family into the woodwork in order to keep their heritage from putting their lives in jeopardy. The young Soros was thus put to work for the Nazis and given a false identity that had been purchased by his father.

Survival over the next year was arduous as George lived in the shoes of a stranger. He posed as the son of a non-Jewish government official and kept his head down for the remainder of the war. The next year felt like an entire lifetime to the young Soros, but by 1945 the war had officially ended and Allied forces began to disassemble the Nazi war machine. George went back to school as if the whole episode had been a dream. Having lived through one of the most difficult periods of the twentieth century, he and his classmates were extraordinarily mature for their ages.

Due to the uncertainty involved in the rebuilding of the Hungarian government, many people in Budapest wondered whether they should move from their ancestral grounds to the greener pastures of the west. Many people resisted the idea, hoping that Budapest would make a comeback and be a better and more secure place to live. However, Soros knew that he had to leave in order to make his way in life. As soon as he finished high school, he decided to leave his country behind and move to London.

## GOING TO SCHOOL IN LONDON

In 1947, Soros enrolled at the London School of Economics (LSE). He knew that the LSE, one of the world's foremost institutions for the study of social sciences, would be the perfect place to reconcile his experiences and expand his horizons.

Soros had already had extensive experience living under dictatorial rule, first at the hands of the Nazis and then at the hands of the communists. He was excited and nervous about moving to England, a place that had an entirely different philosophy of governance. Although many in the West might take democracy for granted, it can be a strange adjustment for someone who has never thought outside of their box. Regardless of what he would find, Soros knew that his real-world experiences offered an awesome perspective to apply to the academia he would find at the LSE.

While in England Soros began a lifelong fascination with philosophy. Of particular influence was Karl Popper's work *The Open Society and Its Enemies*, which introduced the idea of "open" versus "closed" societies. Popper believed that these two cultural paradigms could be used to describe all groups of people. "Closed" societies forced everyone to believe the same thing, whereas "open" societies allowed their inhabitants to formulate their own opinions, free from national bounds. Popper's work was the perfect framework to help Soros put his personal experiences into an intellectual context.

Soros saw his dictator-ridden homeland as an example of a closed society, one in which people simply were unwilling or unable to look past the context in which they were brought up to believe as truth. However, Soros knew that his move to England had allowed him to transition into an open society, where he felt free to think and act as he wanted to. Later in his career, Soros would return to his homeland in order to help spread the word of open societies in order to help more people transition into what he saw as a better way to live.

His intense interests in philosophy lead Soros to dream of pursuing a career in academia. However, his grades were not up to par and after a lukewarm relationship with his inspirational mentor, Karl Popper, proved fruitless, Soros became disheartened and considered more realistic career choices.

George's humble background made it difficult to finance his studies, and he struggled through his years at the LSE. He worked a variety of side jobs to help pay for his studies. One Christmas, while working as a railway porter, Soros broke his leg, leaving him unable to work. Due to a technicality, he was unable to collect social welfare and had to rely on charity from the Jewish Board of Guardians, a nonprofit organization in London.

After graduating from the LSE, the 22-year-old Soros had reality sink in. Although he had lingering fantasies of devoting his career to philosophical pursuits, the realities of his dire situation quickly became apparent. His first job out of college was as a handbag salesman in a small coastal town in northern England. He had a terrible time pushing his product, never wanting to convince a customer to buy a handbag when they didn't really need one. The idealistic Soros floundered and eventually returned to London to look for a career path more suited to his talents.

During college, Soros had a great deal of exposure to the world of finance. Although Soros studied philosophy, the LSE is famous for being the top feeder school to the London financial world. Many of George's classmates had already taken positions at large institutions in the City and had relayed stories about the lifestyle that immensely interested the young Soros.

Although he didn't have much experience, Soros blanketed the City with letters begging for the chance to prove his value. After a long search, Soros was finally offered a position as a trainee trader in gold-stock arbitrage for Singer & Friedlander, a boutique investment bank. It was here that Soros got his first taste of the thrill of the financial markets. However, he had difficulty differentiating himself. Although he had already had fantastic life experiences, London was such a world hub that he wasn't that different from his peers.

He became fascinated by the prospect of selling and buying financial securities. However, by his own account, George was largely a failure at his job. By 1956, Soros had reached the limit of what he could do in London. He needed a place where he could find his niche. He headed for New York City.

## WORK IN NEW YORK

As Soros made his move to New York he realized that his dreams of becoming a philosopher would have to be pushed aside, once and for all, for a career in finance. However, Soros quickly found that his background in philosophy was far more applicable than he could have ever imagined. The traditional wisdom of the financial markets dictates that there must be some underlying logic to the pricing of securities.

His mentor, Karl Popper, had inspired Soros to always think about the big picture. Soros knew that the market was not always as predictable as many financial analysts would have one think. However chaotic the market may be, Soros never felt overwhelmed. Through his introspection, he realized that in order to truly master stocks, chaos must be embraced and randomness submitted to.

·

Although he was not very successful in London, his knowledge of the European financial markets immediately set him apart from his American colleagues. This experience allowed Soros to quickly find a job in international arbitrage, a job that entailed buying and selling the same securities in different markets in order to exploit tiny mispricings. Soros quickly realized that his knowledge of the European markets gave him a huge advantage in the New York rat race. The 1950s was long before the glory days of globalized markets, when local financiers had quick and easy access to information about the worldwide marketplace. American institutions had long been interested only in domestic opportunities, but a sense that money might be made over the pond had just begun to buzz as Soros walked into his first job in New York. Soros's experience and contacts throughout Europe proved to be an invaluable asset, quickly allowing him to differentiate himself among his peers and succeed quickly.

In 1959, Soros moved to Wertheim & Co., a firm that focused specifically on trading between London and New York. Already, Soros was doing things in the financial world that were way ahead of his time. His philosophical approach, combined with a local understanding of the European financial landscape, netted him great gains at Wertheim & Co. In 1960, Soros pointed out that the shares of a large insurance company, Allianz, were seriously undervalued. Despite protests from the company's management, Soros wrote a paper outlining his analysis in order to get the rest of the market behind him. Soros was right; in just a short time, shares of Allianz tripled and he made himself and his company a great deal of money.

By 1961, Soros became a naturalized citizen. His first act as an American citizen was to redraft his novel, *The Burden of Consciousness*, which he had first attempted while he was a student at the LSE in London.

By 1963, Soros finally had a draft that he felt confident in sending to his one-time mentor, Karl Popper. However, Popper's lukewarm reception soured Soros's drive to become a renowned philosopher, and he put down his work to concentrate on his career.

## JOINING THE BIG LEAGUES

Soros quickly discovered that his philosophical approach to understanding the markets and his intellect could push him only so far. Inevitably, instinct had to rule the split-second decisions that made up the daily life of an international financier.

While most traders focused on one type of financial transaction, Soros looked at the financial world as a complex system. Unlike much of Wall Street, Soros has never looked at the financial markets as a series of numbers and equations but instead has seen an organism. This living creature is composed of a multitude of interconnected parts, and, while resilient, it cannot survive without its components. Following this metaphor, Soros has always seen himself as keeping a finger on the pulse of the financial markets, using this connection as the driving force for the instinctual decisions that characterized the rest of his career.

It wasn't until the 1960s that Soros became a true player in the global financial markets. After working at Wertheim & Co., Soros moved to a management position at Arnhold & S. Bleichroeder. While there, he launched two offshore funds. Although the fund was initially funded by capital from his private coffers, he quickly attracted European investors.

Soros had set up a hedge fund, which, at the time, was a relatively new type of investment fund open to a limited range of investors. Hedge funds, which had appeared for the first time on Wall Street two decades earlier, are special types of funds open to a limited range of investors and focused on nontraditional, or "alternative," investments.

The concept of a hedge fund started in 1949 when Alfred Winslow Jones set out to find a way to create a financial strategy that could benefit from both the ups and downs of the market. After setting up a fund, Jones used leverage to buy as many long shares as he could. In order to minimize his losses in the event of a market slide, Jones hedged his position by shorting an equal number of shares. In order to avoid many of the requirements laid out in the Investment Company Act of 1940, Jones limited the membership in his fund to a set of 99 wealthy individuals in a limited partnership. Jones set up a fee structure in which he would take a share of the profits every year. In order to keep the fund desirable, he made it so that he would not take any fee unless he turned a profit.

Over the next few decades, the popularity of hedge funds fluctuated dramatically. When Soros set up his first two funds in 1967, he was certainly going off the beaten path. Once more, Soros decided to exclude Americans from his clientele—he knew that he could raise enough money from his contacts in Europe.

By the mid-1970s Soros was beginning to gain critical acclaim in the wider financial community. He had a long career under his belt and a track record for understanding the subtleties of the international financial marketplace. Not all of the attention on Soros's ability was strictly positive. In the late 1970s the SEC brought what would be the first of many charges against the legendary trader. The allegation was that Soros drove the price of a stock down dramatically the day before a public offering.

Allegedly, this market manipulation occurred when Soros pressured a broker to sell a large order of shares all at once. The SEC had no case, but to avoid the cost of fighting the regulatory giant in court, Soros signed a document that neither admitted nor denied the charges and paid the $1 million fine. In a subsequent interview, Soros implied that the SEC had come after him simply because they were unable to believe that he was able to return such great profits in such a short time.

Despite his prevalence in financial communities, Soros stayed off the radar of the major media outlets. He believed that attracting publicity can be problematic and even bad luck for a fund manager.

## FINDING HIMSELF

During the late 1970s, the Soros Fund was doing amazingly. Though Soros had grown up in a loving home where his parents had loved and nurtured him, he did not return the same type of devotion to his own family. With so many hours at the office, Soros had very little time to nurture his relationship with his wife and children.

By the end of the 1970s, Soros's marriage fell apart and by 1988 he was separated from his wife. On the very day of his separation, he met Susan Weber, the woman who would become his second wife. It was around this time that Soros began to find the limit of his capabilities. His fund had grown so large that he had to hire a great number of employees. All of a sudden, the financial guru was not at the center of his organization, and he was forced to delegate much of the responsibilities for the fund to others. By many accounts, this was where Soros found his limits as a businessperson. Much of what had made him such a successful investor was based on his instinct and tacit knowledge, and he found it was difficult to impart it to his employees.

Jimmy Rogers, a longtime partner of Soros's, was equally dismayed at the prospect of increasing the size of the organization. Rogers spent more time on managing employees than on managing the fund. However, Soros wanted to push forward with expansion, a decision that caused a rift in their partnership and culminated in Rogers's departure from the firm in 1980. This schism had a huge effect on Soros's abilities. With the weight of a large organization crushing down on his shoulders, Soros began to feel burned out. He began to lose the logically detached touch that had turned him into one of the world's greatest financiers, and his investing ability was negatively affected.

One downside of Soros's blind commitment to his analysis is that on the rare occasion that he is wrong, his investors pay dearly. Between 1979 and 1981, Soros took on a heavily leveraged position to bet against the U.S. economy. This short-sighted bet on the bond market turned out to be mistimed, and the market soared, costing Soros's investors close to $80 million in only a few months (see Figure 7.2). It turned out that Soros was off by only a few months; soon the market tanked. Soros was crushed, but he knew that he had to soldier on. This wavering of financial acumen caused many investors to become extremely worried; several investors even pulled money from the fund.

These events shocked Soros into the realization that he needed to find somebody that could help manage the fund. He had taken it as far as he could on his own and needed to finally relinquish some control. Although Soros often remained in the center of the action, he had become focused on his charitable work in Eastern Europe and the Soviet Union and was not willing to handle the day-to-day operations of his Quantum Fund.

Starting in 1982, Soros offloaded much of the fund management responsibilities to a new partner, Victor Niederhoffer. Niederhoffer was a dynamo investor and had created a great deal of returns for the investors of Quantum Fund. However, only a few years after being named a fund

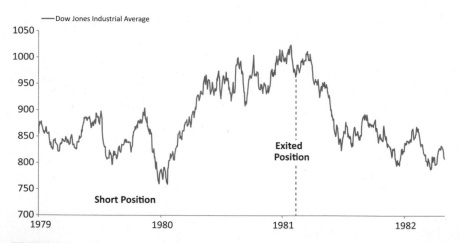

**FIGURE 7.2** An $80 Million Hiccup
*Source:* Historical data from Yahoo! Finance

manager, Niederhoffer decided to branch out on his own, deciding that he craved more independence.

## CRASHING FROM SUCCESS

The 1980s was a dramatic period on Wall Street. Swinging back from a recession in the early part of the decade, investors spent much of the decade making record profits as international markets opened up in eastern Asia and domestic industries were deregulated. In 1986 alone, Soros's Quantum Fund went up by over 40 percent, netting the master financier a $200 million bonus.

Soros felt enthusiastic about this direction of the global marketplace. Bullish investors had pushed the Dow Jones from a low of 776 in 1982 to over 2,700 by the middle of 1987. Quantum Fund had ridden this wave of optimism and had grown to over a billion dollars (see Figure 7.3).

Despite his success, riding this market never sat well with Soros. Much of the success of this period was driven by the reduction of government involvement in the markets, a policy that Soros had always been against. Soros knew that the growth he was experiencing was unsustainable and that it was only a matter of time before the market corrected itself.

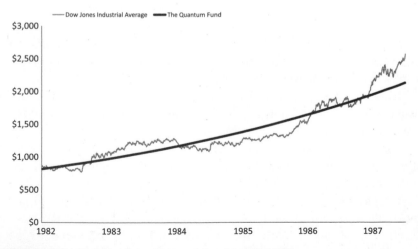

**FIGURE 7.3**  Growth of the Quantum Fund in the 1980s
*Source:* Historical data from Yahoo! Finance

Despite his cognitive dissonance, the public face of Soros remained confident in the ability of his fund to continue returning capital gains to investors. In an interview with *Fortune* magazine during that period, Soros was quoted as saying that just because "stocks have moved up, up and away from the fundamental measures of value does not mean they must tumble."

Soros knew that despite the overvaluation of domestic equities, it was still possible for prices to rise much further. To prove this, Soros looked to the Japanese marketplace. When compared with their fundamental values, Japanese stocks were overpriced by about twice as much as American stocks, yet the market continued to rally.

Soros became extremely worried about the stability of the Tokyo stock market, which led him to pull all of his investor's money out of Japan and funnel it into America. This turned out to be one of the most destructive business decisions of Soros's career.

On October 19, 1987, Soros was suddenly and dramatically ejected from his prediction models as the New York market crashed a record 508 points. Believing this to be the beginning of the apocalyptic economic crash that he had been predicting for years, Soros quickly sold off as many of his long positions as possible. Market makers were more than happy to take the deeply discounted securities off the hands of Soros, who believed that the worse was still yet to come. On Thursday of the same week, prices snapped back into place, netting millions for the traders that covered Soros when he dumped his stocks.

After the smoke cleared, Soros's investors were astonished to discover that he had lost over $200 million in a single day. As can be seen in Figure 7.3, Soros dumped his position after the market bottomed out on October 19. His models predicted that the economy would continue to spiral downward, but it instead leveled out (see Figure 7.4).

Although it seemed as though Soros had been blind to the market swing, he remained extraordinarily confident in his abilities. He would later comment that he had predicted the crash; he just thought that it was going to happen in Japan instead of America. The remainder of October did not offer any relief to Quantum Fund. By the end of the month, the press reported that had lost upward of $800 million in only a few weeks.

Despite this setback, Soros remained incredibly logical and optimistic about the direction of his fund. He reminded his investors that even after all of the October loses, the fund was still up by 2.5 percent for the year. However, the press hung Soros out to dry, printing that he had been one of the biggest losers in the Wall Street crash. Not only did the

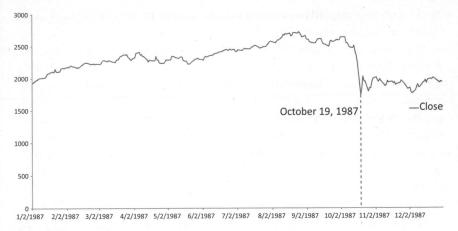

**FIGURE 7.4**  The Crash That Proved Soros Wrong
*Source:* Historical data from Yahoo! Finance

broadsheets report on what happened, but they also made it seem much, much worse.

Despite losing $800 million, Soros adamantly believes that actual losses were about half that. He went on an exhaustive campaign against what he saw as press hysteria, but to no avail. After several months, Soros gave up and vowed never to cooperate with the press again.

These events made Soros come to a critical realization—he needed to find a permanent replacement for himself as the fund manager. With many of his partners having been squeezed out or moved on to their own pursuits, Soros needed a new protégé that he could trust to take his fund to the next level. In 1988, Soros found his new manager, Stanley Druckenmiller.

## A NEW PROTÉGÉ

Soros has had many partners over the years, but none stand out quite as much as the legendary Stanley Druckenmiller. A billionaire in his own right, Druckenmiller helped create many of the financial strategies that projected Soros's Quantum fund along its path of greatness.

Druckenmiller had started his career at the Pittsburg National Bank after dropping out of a Ph.D. program at the University of Michigan. Starting as an analyst, he quickly made his way up the career ladder and within a year was named head of the bank's equity research group. A year later in 1981, he founded his own fund, dubbed Duquesne Capital Management, which he would manage until 2010.

Druckenmiller had developed a complex trading philosophy that was very similar to that of Soros. However, the beginning of the relationship was extremely strenuous. Although Soros immediately referred to Druckenmiller as his "successor," Druckenmiller quickly discovered that he was not the first. In fact, in a short period leading up to the hiring of Druckenmiller, Soros had gone through at least a dozen managers who didn't last more than a few months. To make matters worse, Druckenmiller had developed a taste for independence while running his own fund. Soros, on the other hand, had no intention of letting Druckenmiller loose with the company that he had spent his career building.

Although Druckenmiller spent his first year with his head down, the relationship soon erupted in an open quarrel in which Soros went behind Druckenmiller's back to undermine a business decision. However, the fight proved cathartic for the relationship, and Soros agreed to give Druckenmiller more freedom. In addition, the tumultuous times of Eastern Europe during the early 1990s kept Soros away from New York, allowing Druckenmiller to finally make some returns independently from Soros's hawk-like eye.

## ONTO THE WORLD STAGE

Despite his new found emphasis on his social work, Soros was never far from the action. In 1992, shortly after his philanthropic works began, Soros made a longshot bet that turned out to be one of the most profitable of his entire career.

For over 200 years, the Bank of England had stood as a symbol of monetary stability in the international markets. However, the European regulatory framework had gone through dramatic flux in recent years. No longer on the gold standard, the British pound had, for some time, been on its own against a sea of speculative currency investors. Despite its resilience, many European currencies had not fared quite as well.

This prompted a move toward the Exchange Rate Mechanism (ERM) system, which was designed to be the first move toward a single European currency and a stable monetary system. However, this system required that all of the European countries involved work together. Effectively, this meant that countries with stronger monetary systems would be responsible for weaker ones. Even if a country's fiscal difficulties were its own fault, the stronger governments in the union would be responsible for bailing them out.

The early 1990s were a difficult time for many Eastern European countries. After the collapse of the Soviet Union and Berlin Wall, the newly formulated Eastern European countries had a long way to work toward a stable fiscal system. This left England in an extremely awkward position, as the ERM system force the British government to subsidize the weaker economies.

Soros knew the latent risks involved in this change presented an awesome investment opportunity. Soros believed that despite the political rhetoric, the ERM system would never be able to maintain a unified European economic stance and that stronger systems like Britain would be inevitably forced to abandon the policy.

Soros increased his bet against the pound. When Britain entered a recession, Soros knew that his long-term prediction had come to pass. Britain would be forced to stop subsidizing other countries for its own well-being.

Monetary critics in London began to petition the government to change its mind and leave the ERM. Despite the pressure against the pound, the British prime minister, John Major, doggedly defended England's support of the ERM. Business leaders began to chime in, demanding a realignment of monetary policy in order to drag the country out of its recession.

Again, British politicians blindly stood behind their place in the union. As tension mounted, other funds began to bet against the pound. Soros had sensed a ticking time bomb for years; he just didn't know when it was set to explode. All in all, Soros had more than $10 billion bet against the pound. Ironically, during this entire ordeal, John Major was working on the Maastricht treaty, which would eventually form what is now known as the European Union.

On September 16, 1992, a day that became known as Black Wednesday, the British government finally conceded defeat. Shortly after a last-ditch effort to buy back $26 billion worth of pounds, the British government declared that it was forced to leave the ERM (see Figure 7.5)

Soros had made the right bet, and in a single day he netted over $2 billion for his fund—$1 billion from the pound and $1 billion from his speculations elsewhere in Europe. To the investing world, Soros looked like a god. Many investors made a profit that day; Paul Tudor Jones made $250 million. But nobody had bet so much for so long as Soros.

**FIGURE 7.5**   Onto the World Stage
*Source:* Historical data from Oanda

## The Backlash

Although his bet made the investors of Quantum fund ecstatic, much of the world was enraged. The morning after Black Wednesday, newspapers throughout the world printed stories about how a New York investor made a billion dollars off of the economic woes of Britain. A front-page exposé in London's Daily Mail read "I Made a Billion as the Pound Crashed," featuring a full-page image of a smiling George Soros.

With lingering feelings of contempt toward the press, Soros was reluctant to state his own side of the story to the public. But the media frenzy was too intense. Soros was, for the first time, thrust into the international spotlight, and he needed a voice of his own. Anatole Kaletsky, who was the economics editor of the *Times* of London, was that voice. Kaletsky received a late-night call from a frantic Soros offering him an exclusive interview. Soros's London home had been under siege by a mix of media and protestors for days, and he knew that he had to clear the air around his billion-dollar bet against the pound.

Much of the London media was perturbed by Soros's gains while the British pound fell through the floor. For the first time in years, Soros had decided to state his own story. Kaletsky's ensuing article was one of Soros's first steps to introduce himself to the international community. Although he had been reclusive up to this point, he felt that it was time for him to let the world know that he was here to stay.

## A CONFLICTED MIND

It would seem as though anyone who had amassed a fortune of over $14 billion would be decidedly pro laissez-faire (i.e., free-market capitalism). However, Soros has long been an outspoken advocate of a more mixed economy, with a "strong central. . . . government to correct for the excesses of self-interest." It is ironic, given his net worth. Indeed, Soros has been at the center of financial transactions that have been blamed for being contributing factors to both the 1997 Asian debt crisis and the 1992 UK currency crisis.

Soros's perception of himself as a great predictor of the world's economy led him to publish his first novel, *The Alchemy of Finance*. In this book, Soros outlined his projection of the decline of the American economy. Soros believed that the economic factors driving American capitalism had pushed the country to the edge of its stability. He views himself as this great predictor of the world's economy.

## A NEW ERA

Following the crash of the British pound, Soros began to think that there must be more to life than investing. Despite an illustrious career in the financial markets, he had never quite let go of his aspirations of social philosophy. On his way to becoming the richest man in America, Soros decided that it was time to change his focus to promoting his philosophy of open societies in Eastern Europe and the Soviet Union. With Druckenmiller at the reigns of the Quantum fund, Soros spent more time concentrating on his charitable works in Eastern Europe.

Soros' Open Society Institute and national Soros Foundations have facilitated his giving away a total of between $4 billion and $7 billion of his personal wealth. These organizations have focused on taking education to Eastern Europe in order to help open eyes to the available knowledge of the world. Additionally, Soros has been a fundamental proponent of the Millennium Promise, an organization dedicated to eliminating extreme poverty in Africa. Soros recently pledged $50 million to the cause and continues to do footwork on its behalf.

## RECREATING SOROS'S TRADING STRATEGIES

Soros's skepticism over the stability of the European monetary union helped net his fund one of the largest paydays in recent memory. Despite the gaping holes in the logic behind an amalgamated European financial landscape that were exposed by Soros, the systemic trends have remained unchanged.

In fact, on the same night that the British press were scrambling to report on the American investor who made a billion dollars on the woes of a nation, John Major was negotiating the Maastricht treaty, which eventually formed the European Union. Since its inception, the EU has been extremely problematic. The underlying requisite of a single currency among nations is that each respective government must make fiscal policy that is in the best interest of the whole, rather than focusing on its own constituents. Although nice in theory, this system equates to stronger nations taking up the slack left by countries that are less able to take care of themselves.

For a politician, this means that you need to tell your voting public that you are putting their interests below the interests of (many times) irresponsible foreigners, which can be an extremely difficult proposition. This has caused additional long-range volatility in the price of the pound (which is heavily correlated with the euro) when compared with the U.S. dollar (Figure 7.6).

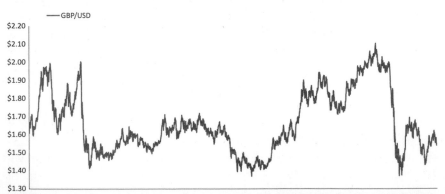

**FIGURE 7.6**  Instability of the European Monetary Union
*Source:* Historical data from Oanda

The massive buildup and crash of the British pound that occurred over the past few years would fit nicely into Soros's models. Greece, Italy, and Spain had dramatically increased their sovereign debt in order to pay for a range of entitlement programs. Effectively, local politicians had started to allow their people to live off the money of other nations, and it was starting to catch up with them. By the middle of 2009, these systems had become unsustainable, and the countries teetered on the edge of bankruptcy. By 2010, Greece began to default on its obligations.

Based on Soros's methodology, this situation would have been perfect to make astronomical returns. The drop in prices could have yielded even more to his investors than his fateful trade in the early 1990s. Germany, as the most economically stable nation at the time, begrudgingly came to the rescue of Greece. Angela Merkel, the German prime minister, was not happy about having to act as the European Union's emergency bank account. Despite the objections of many of her constituents, however, she proceeded as planned.

This type of crisis will undoubtedly happen again. Until the European Union centralizes its government and amalgamates its culture, it will be almost impossible to control differential fiscal policies from conflicting. Until the countries get their act together, hedge fund managers like Soros will be there to happily take a spread.

## SOROS'S TOP TRAITS

Soros has had an amazing life building up his fund. Based in academia, the philosophies that have driven his trading strategies have become legendary; hopeful financiers around the world pore over his every novel in hope of absorbing some modicum of the trading guru's methods. His life has been about more than making money, though. Coming from a tumultuous upbringing, Soros has long focused on helping the downtrodden peoples of the world.

Soros has built a career on making long-range predictions that ended up having gigantic payoffs for his investors. The methodology he used to find and take advantage of these opportunities can be summed up in three trading secrets:

1. *Patience:* Many of Soros's most profitable trades required a superhuman level of patience. To avoid signaling the timing of his intentions

to the marketplace, Soros had to build his position over the course of several years. This meant that Soros had to remain confident in the original assessment of the position in the face of often contradictory evidence from many different directions.

2. *Persistence:* Soros's most profitable trades were always against the best wisdom of the marketplace. He knew that if he found an opportunity that had not yet been identified by other investors, he could make a great return for his fund. However, going against the grain of the marketplace can take a real toll on a fund manager. A big part of Soros's competitive advantage has been his ability to look directly at the market and hold steady to his positions, even in the face of adversity and/or financial ruin. This logical steadfastness has given Soros the tools to stick to the trades that he knows are moneymakers and continually return abnormally high profits to his investors.

3. *Pulling the Trigger*: What is important to understand is that you need to put your money where your mouth is. Anyone can speculate on markets and become a millionaire on paper. Putting real money into a market and taking it out for a profit is an entirely different thing. Soros had the courage and financial prowess to do just this.

■  ■  ■

Next up, we'll review how Greenlight Capital's David Einhorn ruffled the feathers of the investment world.

# CHAPTER 8

# David Einhorn

## A Company's Worst Nightmare

D avid Einhorn is the epitome of the activist hedge fund manager. Any company he is looking to short had better brace itself for headwinds.

The 43-year-old Einhorn is the founder of hedge fund Greenlight Capital, which he purportedly started with $1 million of his own money in 1996. Einhorn's fund has become one of the most successful and well-known hedge funds in the business with around $6 billion in assets under management at the beginning of 2011.

His success story revolves around two famous trades that are similar to others made in this book. His shorting of Allied Capital was popular and well-known in the same way that Jim Chanos shorted Enron stock.

The other trade is his short selling of doomed financial institution Lehman Brothers. During the collapse of Lehman, Einhorn actively petitioned the firm to explain what he saw as improper markings of collateralized debt obligation (CDO) values in Lehman's books. His persistence ultimately paid off, leaving him with a handsome reward for his troubles.

## ALLIED IS NOT AN ALLY

David Einhorn has made multiple trades and bets throughout his career, but two stand out and were highly publicized. The first big trade involved his crusade against a company called Allied Capital, a private-equity firm

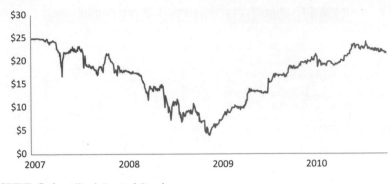

**FIGURE 8.1**   Allied Capital Stock
*Source:* Historical data from Yahoo! Finance

and capital markets participant that traded under the ticker ALD up until its 2010 acquisition by Ares Capital Corporation in April 2010. (See Figure 8.1.)

Like Chanos and his investigation into Enron, Einhorn looked into the business and financials of Allied. What he saw didn't make sense. Allied Capital wasn't properly stating the amount of its assets on the books and wasn't marking down losses.

Thus began the personal quest of Einhorn to prove that Allied Capital was a dud. He began shorting the stock in 2002 and continued to do so up until 2008 or so when the credit crunch caused Allied Capital to essentially go out of business as its value plummeted along with its assets.

It first became known that Einhorn was short Allied in May 2002, when he gave a speech at the Ira W. Sohn Investment Research Conference, an annual conference where the brightest and best fund managers in the business convene every year and discuss investments, finance, and strategy. Einhorn has been a repeat guest since 2002.

His speech detailed why he believed Allied was a fraud and that he was shorting the stock. He recommended that conference attendees do the same. The next day, the New York Stock Exchange halted the stock after it dropped nearly 20 percent in intraday trading.

Einhorn was generally incensed by the activities going on inside many Wall Street firms. His complaints ranged from manipulation of the Small Business Administration to favoritism between banks and other financial institutions.

What happened over the following years would be a drawn-out battle that would involve Einhorn and Greenlight Capital, Allied Capital, and the Securities and Exchange Commission. Einhorn complained to the SEC about Allied's alleged misdoings, and Allied in turn claimed that Einhorn was purposely making up false statements in order to drive down the company's share price, thus benefiting his short position.

The SEC investigated Einhorn over allegations that he manipulated the company's share price, but nothing ever stuck. In 2007, however, the SEC decided to finally act on Einhorn's claims that Allied was a fraud. The *New York Times* wrote:

> *[In June 2007] the S.E.C. found that Allied violated record-keeping and internal-controls provisions of securities laws relating to the valuation of illiquid securities it held. In a settlement, Allied neither admitted nor denied the allegations; not a nickel in fines or penalties was assessed.*[1]

The similarities between Einhorn and Chanos are uncanny. Both did their detective work long before either company was accused of any major wrongdoings. They then began a position and held their ground even as share prices fluctuated and continued to do so until they were proven right by U.S. regulatory and judicial agencies.

But what is interesting about Einhorn's story is what he did with the profits from Allied Capital. The exact amount is unknown, but seeing as how Greenlight Capital went from $1 million in assets under management to several billion over the course of a short time, we can only assume it was a healthy profit.

Greenlight Capital has originally sought to donate half of all profits from the Allied short to the Ira Sohn Research Conference Foundation, which provides funding to local pediatric cancer treatment and maintenance organizations. Seeing as how his profits took a long time to materialize, he then gave $1 million to the foundation in 2005. He would donate $7 million to the foundation by the end of 2009.

As for Allied Capital, the company's stock plummeted into penny-stock range during the credit crisis of 2008 after trading in the midteens a year earlier. It was acquired by Ares Capital in 2010 for an undisclosed sum, but some details of how much debt Allied was in can be found in an April 1, 2010, press release on Ares Capital's web site:

> *At closing, Ares Capital retired in full Allied Capital's $250 million senior secured term loan arranged by J.P. Morgan Securities Inc. on January 29, 2010. Ares Capital also assumed all of Allied Capital's*

*other outstanding debt obligations, including approximately $745 million in Allied's publicly traded unsecured notes. As previously disclosed, Ares Capital's revolving commitments increased by $75 million to $690 million with the closing of the Allied merger.*[2]

The dirty details of Einhorn's long fight with Allied Capital were published in the book, *Fooling Some of the People All of the Time: A Long Short Story* penned by Mr. Einhorn himself (John Wiley & Sons, 2008).

Though the battle with Allied Capital was the first major victory for Einhorn, it wouldn't be his last.

## LUCKY LEHMAN

While only a handful of hedge fund managers were lucky enough to bank a large amount of coin from the financial crisis, people mentioned in this book like Paulson and Bass were short the housing crisis. Einhorn, however, decided to go after Lehman Brothers (see Figure 8.2).

Einhorn's battle with Lehman goes beyond a simple hunch and initiating a position or simply getting lucky. It goes back to 2007, when like a few other hedge fund managers and speculators, Einhorn believed Lehman had two main issues.

The first issue was that he believed the firm was greatly undercapitalized. While it may seem completely obvious now after the movies and

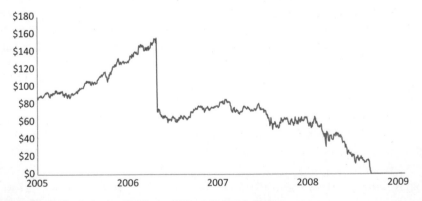

**FIGURE 8.2**  Lehman Brothers Historical Stock Price
*Source:* Historical data from Yahoo! Finance

books written about Lehman's dire financial situation, Einhorn must have done his homework. (Lehman's problems with its creditors are still being sorted out as of this writing.)

The other issue is that Lehman was not being straight with its bookkeeping. Taking a cue from Enron, it was shuffling illiquid assets onto off-balance-sheet, special purpose vehicles (SPVs) that would hold the crummy assets until after quarterly reporting periods at which point Lehman would "buy" the assets back from the SPV and put them back on the books.

"Repo 105" is the most famous transaction that leaked out of Lehman after its demise, exposing just how fraudulent the firm's activities were under the reign of chief executive Dick Fuld. As the *New York Times* explains, the deal was scandalous:

> *According to the report, Lehman used what amounted to financial engineering to temporarily shuffle $50 billion of assets off its books in the months before its collapse in September 2008 to conceal its dependence on leverage, or borrowed money. Senior Lehman executives, as well as the bank's accountants at Ernst & Young, were aware of the moves.*[3]

Early on, Einhorn saw Lehman at its true value and chose to go after the company by shorting its stock. In April 2008, Einhorn and Greenlight Capital called Erin Callan, the chief financial officer of Lehman Brothers. The two discussed what Einhorn alleged were discrepancies in the firm's accounting and other irregularities. He figured he would give Callan a chance to explain herself.

Einhorn later told *New York Magazine* that Callan was "evasive" and "dishonest" in their conversation and that it reminded him of his battle with Allied Capital.[4]

As he had with Allied Capital, Einhorn called on regulators to go after Lehman and examine its accounting practices and ensure that the firm was well capitalized. Though the Federal Reserve and Treasury Department eventually got around to dealing with Lehman in the midst of the financial crisis, it was already too late. The firm was toast and Einhorn had won.

Eventually, Callan was fired after Einhorn went public with his conversation that he had with her, which in turn drove down the price of Lehman's stock substantially. Lehman Brothers filed for bankruptcy and, unlike Bear Stearns, did not enjoy the luxury of a government-sponsored bailout.

## THE GREAT BEYOND

Since Lehman and Allied, Einhorn has remained busy with Greenlight Capital and other activities. He remains a shrewd gambler and not just in the stock market. Einhorn is known for his ability to hold his own in both poker and bridge, in 2006 bringing home an impressive $660,000 from the World Series of Poker, which is held in Las Vegas each year.

As far as his ventures with Greenlight Capital go, Einhorn currently isn't on any crusades (as of this writing, anyway), but that could always change. The most recent filing with the SEC is a Form 13F-HR filed in February 2011. From the look of it, Einhorn's possible next big bets are on companies like Apple and Sprint-Nextel.

Some of Greenlight's biggest holdings from the filing include:

- *Becton, Dickinson and Co. (Ticker: BDX):* A global medical technology company engaged in the development, manufacture, and sale of medical devices, instrument systems and reagents used by health-care institutions, life science researchers, clinical laboratories, the pharmaceutical industry and the general public.
- *CareFusion Corporation (Ticker: CFN):* A global medical technology company specializing in product lines in the areas of IV infusion, medication and supply dispensing, respiratory care, infection prevention, and surgical instruments.
- *Einstein Noah Restaurant Group, Inc. (Ticker: BAGL):* A food company that operates under the Einstein Bros. Bagels (Einstein Bros.), Noah's New York Bagels (Noah's), and Manhattan Bagel Company (Manhattan Bagel) brands.
- *MI Developments Inc. (Ticker: MIM):* A real estate operating company engaged in the acquisition, development, construction, leasing, management, and ownership of an industrial rental portfolio leased primarily to Magna and its automotive operating units.
- *Microsoft Corporation (Ticker: MSFT):* One of the most well-known corporations globally, Microsoft has five business divisions: Windows & Windows Live Division, Server and Tools, Online Services Division, Microsoft Business Division, and Entertainment and Devices Division.
- *Pfizer Inc. (Ticker: PFE):* Research-based, global biopharmaceutical company and drug juggernaut.
- *Sprint Nextel Corporation (Ticker: S):* One of the big four cellphone carriers. Also operates and owns a stake in Clearwire, a 4G wireless service provider.

Clearly, diversification is a big part of Einhorn's strategy. It appears that he is also big on technology at the moment, which could pay off big considering that companies like Facebook are receiving astronomical valuations. To me, it looks like we're in the midst of another 2000-era dot-com bubble, but this type of market could end up being the norm now that the Dow Jones Industrial Average is above 13,000 and the S&P 500 is trading above 1,300.

For now, being long is a good thing for Greenlight Capital and its investors. As long as Ben Bernanke and the Federal Reserve keep the policy of quantitative easing in place, it is pretty safe to say that despite occasional dips and corrections, stocks will continue to go higher. What will be interesting to see is whether the technology sector can keep pace with the market.

## RECREATING EINHORN'S TRADING STRATEGIES

Throughout this chapter, I have made numerous comparisons between Jim Chanos and David Einhorn. While Chanos is known in investment circles as a permabear (i.e. a big short-seller), Einhorn is generally long equities save for the two spectacular tales told previously.

To act like Einhorn and to trade like Einhorn, you must first begin to *think* like Einhorn. You need to find a company that grabs your attention. Maybe it rubs you the wrong way. Maybe it came out with an earnings report that seemed too good to be true. Perhaps you just think the CEO is incompetent. Whatever your reason, start with that and dig deeper.

The SEC is your friend, believe it or not. All corporate filings with the publicly traded company that you've honed in on will be listed on its web site. Search through documents using the EDGAR tool, www.sec.gov/edgar.shtml. Quarterly earnings reports are always important to look through as companies provide future guidance and like to bury footnotes with unsavory information.

Initiating a short position is as simple as calling up your broker and borrowing the stock from them. However, start small. Don't risk more than 2 percent of your available capital in your position. Should your thesis begin to pay off, add to your position in increments. Don't bet the house unless you have concrete proof that the company you're about to short is beyond redemption, and even then hedge accordingly.

Though it may be hard to find a company similar to Lehman in a world where the Dodd-Frank Act reigns over big banks, there will be plenty of opportunities to rally against a firm like Allied Capital. All you need to do is find some kind of discrepancy that doesn't sit right with you.

Buy 100 shares of the company you've chosen to go after so you become a shareholder. As a shareholder, call up the company's management and demand that they explain the discrepancy to you. Take meetings with them. Badger them if you must. Their fiduciary obligation is to appease you, the shareholder. Fight for your right to know what's going on behind their closed doors.

Financial companies may seem like the usual suspects when it comes to finding a shady company to short, but that's not always the case. Companies like Tyco and Enron were full of corruption, and more recently a few Chinese companies listed on the New York Stock Exchange have become an easy target. The argument is that most of the Chinese companies have done a reverse merger—buying a cheap, NYSE-listed company to become public in the United States while sidestepping many checks and balances.

China MediaExpress Holdings Inc. (Ticker: CCME) has become the poster child for these sorts of companies, experiencing a huge decline in its share price after a research firm called Muddy Waters issued a report calling the business an outright fraud. Despite being audited by power accounting firm Deloitte (which has since cut the firm loose), the damage has been done and many have moved on to other Chinese companies listed on NYSE, trying to find the next CCME.

It goes to show that if you start with an idea and shout loud enough from your soapbox like Muddy Waters did, you can make a huge impact in the market. Whether or not Muddy Waters held a short position in CCME remains to be seen, as manipulating the market for your own benefit is something the SEC frowns upon.

## EINHORN'S TOP TRAITS

One can argue that David Einhorn is the epitome of an activist fund manager. These traits make him stand out among the other thousands of fund managers on the buy side:

- *Be an activist:* I can't stress this enough. Don't take any excuses from a company that you have a short position in. Let the world know what your thesis is and encourage them to join your cause. Rebuke management for documents and make them answer your questions. Record your phone calls or, at the very least, transcribe them. If management gives you any trouble, air out the dirty laundry in public.

- *Mix things up:* Surely you've heard the adage "don't put all your eggs in one basket." While you may have a massive short position on one stock, the market may be in the midst of a bull rally or vice versa. Go with the flow. Make sure your portfolio isn't totally correlated to U.S. equity markets. Throw some commodities, Treasuries, and bonds into the mix for good measure. If the market gets volatile, get some exposure to the VIX via an ETF or the futures. It's up to you to be a good investor. Money doesn't just fall into one's lap.

- *Set a good example for others:* Know why other hedge fund managers respect David Einhorn and Greenlight Capital? It's not just because he's a good stock picker or believes in his cause. It's the other things he does, like donating proceeds of his Allied Capital short to charity, that go a long way with others who believe in the same causes.

- *Know your boundaries:* One could argue (as Allied Capital did) that Einhorn's public denunciation of Allied Capital bordered on market manipulation since he had a position against the company. Make sure that you don't do anything exorbitant (read: illegal) when going on a crusade against a public company. Keep in mind that Einhorn probably had a great legal team backing him up and also had capital to spare in the event of a lawsuit. Chances are that you don't, so be careful.

■ ■ ■

Remember, Greenlight Capital started with almost nothing and turned it-self into a larger, well-respected hedge fund that nearly everyone in the investment community pays attention to. Since its inception, the fund has delivered an annualized return, net of all fees and expenses, of more than 20 percent. That certainly beats putting your money in a savings bond.

Next, we'll examine one of the greatest options and futures traders to ever grace the floor: Martin "Buzzy" Schwartz.

**CHAPTER 9**

# Martin Schwartz

*From Amateur to Superstar*

M artin "Buzzy" Schwartz is the epitome of a trader. He is not a big-league hedge fund manager and, since the 1990s, he has essentially faded into obscurity. No doubt he is enjoying his early retirement brought on by the immense profits he made trading in the 1970s through the 1990s.

What makes Schwartz's story amazing is that many people can relate to it. He was essentially a blue-collar guy who happened to have done well in school, got his MBA, served in the Marines, and then quit his day job to become a trader. Many people share Schwartz's dream, but not everyone will enjoy his success, especially since the markets have changed dramatically since Schwartz's time.

## START SMALL, GO BIG

Schwartz came from a pretty average background. He went to Amherst College in 1967 and from there served in the U.S. Marine Corps Reserves for about five years while studying to get his MBA from Columbia University. He landed a job at E.F. Hutton—a brokerage firm that had been around since Jesse Livermore's time—as a financial analyst.

Being a financial analyst apparently got old quickly. Schwartz soon realized he needed to make more money and do something that excited him. On the advice of a friend, he started looking into trading stocks and decided that he wanted to eventually quit his job and become a trader full time.

One of the things you need to do before you start trading is to save up or raise capital. In a book he wrote in 1999 called *Pit Bull: Lessons from Wall Street's Champion Day Trader*, Schwartz dubbed these savings his "grubstake." The book is essentially an autobiographical history of Schwartz's career as a trader, and I highly recommend giving it a read.

This initial grubstake that Schwartz saved up was $100,000, a pretty decent chunk of money back in 1980s and is still plenty to trade with today. One must realize, however, that he spent $90,000 of that $100,000 to buy a seat or membership on the American Stock Exchange (AMEX) so his trading costs would be lowered.

In *Pitbull*, readers learn about both sides of trading. Schwartz talks about his first experience trading on the floor of the AMEX, which was eventually acquired by the New York Stock Exchange. He takes readers through the entire process of waiting in the member lounge, the vibe of the exchange floor, and how worried he became over his first trades.

Schwartz eventually graduated from the floor to "upstairs"—the term for off-the-floor, nonexchange trading. This is where he crafted his trading style and learned about technical analysis.

One key thing to understand about Schwartz is that like many people in the industry, he had a mentor. Bob Zoellner was a trader in the 1960s and 1970s who was responsible for giving Schwartz guidance and help when he needed it early in his career. They met in 1973 while working together at a small brokerage house called Edwards and Hanly. Zoellner kept the firm alive by actively trading its house account.

Early in his career, Schwartz really relied on Zoellner when he ran into trouble on the AMEX floor. If a position was losing money, he'd call up Zoellner and, as cool as a cucumber, Zoellner would tell him what to do.

Schwartz entered the U.S. Trading Championship in 1983 and placed third in the futures category. In 1984 he won it. He continued to enter year after year by sending in his profit and loss statements, consistently ranking among the top traders in the competition.

The following quote from his book describes Schwartz's mind-set when he decided to enter the competition: "Going for the knockout had made me a loser for nine years. Now that I'd developed a methodology that fit my personality, I was going to stick with it whether I was trading $5000 or $500,000."

Afterward, Schwartz went on to trade other people's money and opened a fund called Sabrina Partners. This didn't work out well for him.

Schwartz was the kind of man who liked to be his own boss, and having to worry about losing other people's money proved too much for him, especially after suffering from a virus that landed him in the hospital three times and required heart surgery. He closed his fund down and went back to trading his own money.

## TRADING LIKE A ROCK STAR

You don't become a great trader without having some kind of secret sauce or special skillset. For Schwartz, this was technical analysis and sticking to trading one product: S&P futures contracts. Figure 9.1 shows a historical chart of the S&P 500 Index. All those little dips you see in the 1970s through the 1990s are how Schwartz made his profits.

During his tenure as a securities analyst, Schwartz used fundamental analysis to influence his trading decisions. This included things like economic data and took on more of a big-picture approach. He eventually switched to technical trading, which is what made him the big bucks.

Technical trading involves studying all aspects of a certain security. One may study price and volume, as Schwartz did, or indicators like the 200-day moving average. You can even get more technical with indicators like Bollinger bands or wave theory.

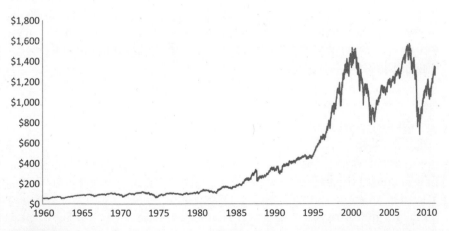

**FIGURE 9.1** Historical Performance of the S&P 500
*Source:* Historical data from Yahoo! Finance

Schwartz engaged in scalping, which means getting in and out of the market multiple times, quickly, and taking multiple amounts of small profits instead of going for a big win. It lowers risk, ensures that you take profits, and works well for people with limited resources. According to Schwartz, this entails cutting losses quickly and closing out winners just as fast.

It also helps to be good with numbers and be a gambler. In my experience, many gamblers I've been acquainted with seem to enjoy the market and are quite good at it. Here's what Schwartz says about his ability to work with numbers:

> *Hard work is the primary reason why I've become so successful but hard work's just part of the equation. By nature, I'm a gambler with a good feel for numbers, and, as I've mentioned before, Amherst taught me how to think, Columbia Business School taught me what to think about, the Marine Corps taught me how to perform under fire, and Audrey taught me the importance of money management.*[1]

Audrey, his wife, influenced him greatly throughout his career; especially when he needed to make a tough call or came to a crossroads and had to decide what to do in regard to his trading.

The most important notion set forth by Schwartz is that *you need to put your money where your mouth is*. This means you need to save up and put money that you can afford to lose in a trading account. You then should try out your methodologies and tactics in the market, with real money. Paper trading is easy for anyone to do—you don't have anything at risk and can always start over again. Real money will prevent you from taking exorbitant, stupid risks and will teach you how to hedge properly, in addition to other techniques.

## WINDING DOWN

Schwartz eventually made a lot of money, which propelled his trading to new heights. In his first year of professional trading, he brought in $600,000. The next year, he did $1.2 million. Compound your profits and reinvest them and suddenly you're a player. That's what happened with Schwartz.

At the end of his career, in his mid-40s, Schwartz ended up in the hospital due to the stress associated with trading. His doctor and therapist both told him he needed to stop trading and, although he slowed things down a bit—he essentially had to and could barely go for a walk outside after his hospitalization—he continued to trade.

Gold also became an important thing for Schwartz. Physical gold is something that Schwartz picked up from his grandfather when he was a child. Later in his life, when he was doing bad in the market or he thought the world was about to end—he was stressed out and was on medicine prescribed by his doctor—he would insist that his wife get their gold bullion from the bank and bring it home. (See Figure 9.2 for the price of gold over the years.)

Schwartz even considered giving up stock trading in favor of commodities trading:

> *I became so fascinated with gold that late in 1979, after I made my first hundred thousand on the Amex, I considered selling my seat and buying one on the New York Commodity Exchange (COMEX). I wanted to become Auric Schwartz, the gold trader. I discussed the idea with Audrey, and we agreed that it wouldn't be such a good idea.*[2]

**FIGURE 9.2** Historical Price of Gold
*Source:* NYMEX

Schwartz's wife gave him sound advice. He should stick with what he's good at: trading stocks. If he wanted exposure to gold, he could always trade gold stocks on the AMEX. This is especially easy nowadays with exchange-traded funds like the SPDR Gold Trust ETF from State Street (Ticker: GLD).

It is rumored that Schwartz is now living in Florida, spending his time trading oil futures and the S&Ps. Whatever he's up to, he's most likely making money hand over fist.

## RECREATING SCHWARTZ'S TRADING STRATEGIES

One distinct advantage that Schwartz had in his trading career was that financial futures were relatively new products when he began trading them. Electronic trading was not as prevalent as it is today and thus more opportunities for arbitrage were available.

Schwartz focused primarily on S&P 500 futures. Whether he traded the "bigs" or large S&P contracts, as opposed to the E-mini contracts that are now offered at the Chicago Mercantile Exchange (CME), is not a concern. You can execute the same strategies without having to risk millions of dollars in capital using the E-minis, which are low-cost (relatively speaking) and are highly liquid contracts. These futures are traded electronically, not on the floor, so you could argue that everyone's on the same playing field.

Having a good overall understanding of global equity markets is really important when trading a futures contract that's linked to one of the world's most popular stock indices. If something happens in Europe, Japan, or China that causes those markets to fall, chances are the S&P as well as the Dow and NASDAQ are going to follow suit.

You should also understand which stocks are parts of the S&P 500 and how they are weighted. Sectors are also important to pay attention to. If technology takes a big hit premarket, you should understand which stocks will get hit the hardest and that perhaps you should short the NASDAQ Composite Index temporarily. You don't have to follow the S&P exclusively.

If you're going to trade indices like Schwartz, you need to have some kind of technological advantage. In Schwartz's memoir, he mentions that when he was trading upstairs or off the floor, he used a Telerate machine to gain an edge over other traders. While the Telerate is now a relic, you too can gain an advantage by focusing on four important parts of your trading setup:

1. *Platform:* You need a good platform. If you're going to be an active trader, make sure you use a robust platform that lets you trade multiple products quickly and efficiently and has all the tools you need and want. Personally, I am a fan of TD Thinkorswim, but there are plenty of other good ones, such as Lightspeed Trader, Livevol, and TradeStation.

2. *Execution:* You may want to work with other traders out of an office or join a proprietary trading shop that can offer you super quick execution. Fast execution means best price and best price means better profits. The lower the latency, the better.

3. *Brokerage:* Your prime broker should offer fantastic prices, great execution, and connectivity that suits your strategy. If you're serious and have a lot of capital, talk to some of the bulge-bracket firms like Goldman Sachs and Morgan Stanley, which have established electronic trading groups. If you're at a lower rung on the ladder, then look into Lightspeed, Lime Brokerage, and similar firms. If you're trading futures or options, a firm that offers lower margin requirements could end up saving you a few bucks and allowing you to stretch you money further.

4. *Strategy:* This one is the most important. Like Schwartz, you too should have a clear-cut strategy of what you're going to trade and how you're going to do it. Don't buy some random pharmaceutical company because your cousin's friend in Queens told you it was a "sure thing." Stick with what you know and understand and slowly expand your knowledge of other products.

## SCHWARTZ'S TOP TRAITS

Acting like Schwartz means you need to dial back the clock a bit and go over the fundamentals of trading. All of these traits may seem obvious but I cannot stress enough how important they are:

- *Don't risk all your capital:* When you first start trading and even if you're somewhat of a veteran, don't plow 50 percent of your available cash into a single position because you think it's going to pay off. What if it doesn't? You're in trouble. A good rule of thumb is to never risk more than 2 percent of your capital on any single trade. That way, even if you mess up, you have plenty of other shots to make that money back and try again.

- *Take a break:* As if it wasn't obvious already, trading can be stressful! It's very easy to lose your cool or become emotional over a position. Don't get bent out of shape; step away from your computer, terminal, phone, or whatever it is you're trading with and take a break. Go for a walk and clear your head, eat lunch, read a book. Whatever works best for relieving stress and getting your mind off of things, go do it for 15 minutes at least and then reevaluate your positions. An emotional trader is more likely to get burned.

- *Follow the rules:* Schwartz had two simple rules for trading and making money, and I suggest you take note: "My first rule was never to risk more than I could afford to lose. My second rule was to try to book a profit every day."

■ ■ ■

Even if you're a beginner, you too can "make it" like Buzzy Schwartz did. Start slow, build up your capital, and trade bigger, all while hedging and keeping the aforementioned traits in mind. If you're good, you'll get to where you want to be soon enough. The markets are always open (save for a few days each year), so don't worry about opportunities passing you by. There will always be new ones around the corner.

Next up, in Chapter 10, we look at one of the most successful energy traders, John Arnold.

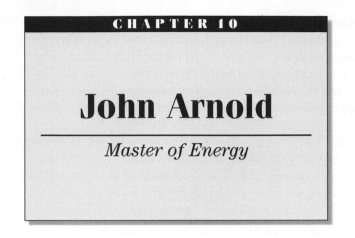

## CHAPTER 10

# John Arnold

*Master of Energy*

You don't have to be a trader or work in the industry to know that energy is a huge business. Just look at your next heating bill or at the gas pump next time you fill up your car.

Oil isn't the only place you can make money. There's big money in solar power, wind energy, and natural gas, among other things. John D. Arnold is a man who hit it big trading natural gas in the 1990s and 2000s, and he went on to found one of the most successful energy trading hedge funds, Centaurus Energy, after leaving Enron. He now ranks as one of the world's richest people with a net worth well over a billion dollars.

## SUCCESS AT ENRON

After reading Chapter 2 on Jim Chanos, you no doubt have a better understanding of how Enron worked and what went wrong with the company. Despite the bad rap that's normally associated with Enron, the company did in fact have a highly successful trading operation and made many of its traders very wealthy.

After graduating from college, Arnold began working at Enron as an energy analyst. He soon moved to trading crude oil and eventually to natural gas. This proved to be his bread and butter, and Arnold began making lots of money for the firm. In one year alone, he brought in $750 million in trading profits, earning an $8 million bonus for his efforts.

While energy is still traded in significant size on the floor with futures contracts and swap derivatives, Enron pioneered online trading with its Enron Online business, giving Arnold a significant advantage and the ability to arbitrage different contracts at different prices. He also acted as a natural gas market maker, which brought in a significant amount of revenue at Enron, but also hurt him, according to the *New York Times:*

> *In 2000, when natural gas prices were rocketing skyward and energy markets were uncommonly volatile, Mr. Arnold had a decidedly un-Ruthian year. He racked up more than $200 million in profit, he says, only to see it vanish by year's end, mainly because of his market-maker role. Internal Enron records show that over all, he lost more than $27 million in 2000.*[1]

No matter. Arnold's huge profits soon made up for the damage done from his market-making operation.

Another significant advantage that Arnold had working at Enron was the fact that Enron was deeply involved in the actual delivery of natural gas with its pipelines business. This kind of information proved critical not just for Arnold, but also for the rest of Enron's energy traders. It's like having a cheat sheet (not actual cheating, but having a wealth of information available at your disposal) when you take a test. You'll probably do very well.

Eventually, Enron collapsed, but before it did, Arnold quit. He made a fortune by working for the company and decided he wanted to be his own boss. In 2002, he founded Centaurus Energy and set out to do what he did best: trading natural gas.

## CENTAURUS ENERGY

Centaurus Energy (also known as Centaurus Advisors) is a Houston-based hedge fund that specializes in natural gas trading. Arnold used money that he made from Enron to seed the fund and get it off the ground.

He also poached some of Enron's best traders and got them to come work with him at the fund. This was a smart move, because if you ask anyone who knows the street how good Enron's traders are, chances are they'll reply: "They *are* good." Those who didn't join Arnold soon went to UBS when the bank bought the remnants of Enron's energy trading operations.

The hedge fund is known for its massive returns since inception. Yearly returns run the gamut from 30 percent to 300 percent, with Arnold's only loss occurring in 2010, when his fund lost 4 percent.

Centaurus deals primarily in speculation, market making in the natural gas industry, and dealing with credit risk among companies. He is heavily involved in over-the-counter energy markets. Arnold explained how this works in a New York Mercantile Exchange (NYMEX) interview from 2005:

> *After Enron collapsed, there was a general revaluation of credit risk among energy companies. The better credits were less willing to take on the lesser credits as counter parties. So the lesser credits found themselves with fewer counter parties willing to trade with them, even though they still needed to hedge the pricing risks in their business.*[2]

And though hedge fund titans like Paulson and Bass foresaw the collapse of the housing market, Arnold bet that commodities would drop in value in 2008 and he made a killing when it happened. It is reported that he reaped in $1 billion in one year sometime between 2002 and 2009.

But after the collapse in 2008, regulators sprung into action. The Commodity Futures Trading Commission or CFTC started talking to speculators and hedgers about their activities in the market in 2009 and the exchanges started imposing position limits to limit the activity of large firms like Arnold's. Arnold testified to the CFTC that NYMEX's position limits would hurt traders in commercial hedging:

> *If the proposed position limits take effect, the commercial hedger would no longer transact with the best buyer/seller, but instead with the best buyer/seller among a narrower universe of participants— those who have less than 1,000 contracts of open interest . . . this will decrease liquidity and increase transaction costs for the commercial hedger.*[3]

NYMEX has yet to relent on position limits, which has hampered Centaurus's profit generation, but it remains to be seen whether the limitations will materially affect Arnold in the long run. Centaurus has been fined multiple times for exceeding position limits, but the fines pale in comparison to the money Arnold is bringing in.

Still, it would be hard to find an opportunity like Arnold did in late 2005 when he took advantage of a large energy-focused hedge fund called Amaranth Advisors.

## THE EXPLOSION

Though Arnold's hedge fund is large, there was once an even larger hedge fund called Amaranth Advisors, which once had as much as $9 billion in assets under management.

Founded in 2000 and located in Greenwich, Connecticut, Amaranth originally dealt in the convertible arbitrage space but soon moved into energy trading and, much like Centaurus, natural gas trading.

Amaranth has an employee named Brian Hunter, a Canadian who was by and large an excellent trader. Hunter earned his keep at Deutsche Bank, doing well on the firm's energy desk for a few years. But in 2003, he had a trade blow up, which ended up costing Deutsche Bank tens of millions of dollars. As I said earlier, natural gas can be quite a volatile market.

Hunter eventually landed at Amaranth, trading natural gas, and was allowed to run his own book. The arrangement was working out fine until 2006, when Hunter made a huge bet during the winter of 2006–2007. He speculated that natural gas prices would rise when in fact, they did quite the opposite: They fell considerably. Amaranth found itself with a $6.6 billion loss and subsequently the firm unwound its positions and closed.

Someone had to take the other side of Amaranth's trades and thus made a winning bet. After all, there are always two parties to derivatives trades. He wasn't the only person who was betting against Hunter, but John Arnold was on the other side making quite a bit of money thanks to Hunter's mistakes. The *Wall Street Journal* paints a picture of how big of a threat Arnold could be in the natural gas market in the mid-2000s:

> *With others they talked to, some Amaranth traders claimed Mr. Arnold was driving gas prices against Amaranth, according to someone who was approached. Their pitch was: We've got one guy in the market trading against us. If you take over our positions and hold onto them, you can make a billion dollars.*[4]

No one except Arnold and a few select others knows the exact amount of profit that he made on the trade against Hunter, but chances are it was a princely sum reserved for one of the world's greatest energy traders. It is said that Centaurus had returns exceeding 150 percent for 2005.

## RECREATING ARNOLD'S TRADING STRATEGIES

Energy is a tricky game. You really need to know your stuff and have a decent-sized operation in order to deal in swaps. But the smaller investor also can make money through crude oil and natural gas trades.

### Crude Oil

One way is to buy or sell futures contracts on exchanges like the New York Mercantile Exchange (NYMEX, now part of CME Group) and InterContinental Exchange (ICE).

Be warned that CME has more than 100 very complex contracts for energy traders, so you should avoid these at all costs. For all intents and purposes, we'll stick with crude oil and natural gas contracts for speculatory purposes.

There are two main types of crude oil: Brent and West Texas Intermediate (WTI). Both are light crude oils, with Brent being lighter than WTI. Instead of getting into the differences, we'll focus strictly on WTI.

If you have a decent amount of capital at your disposal, you can trade WTI Light Sweet Crude Oil futures (CL), which are one of the world's most liquid energy contracts. Should CL contracts prove to be too expensive or the margin requirements too high, check out the E-mini version of these (QM), which is half the size of the standard Light Sweet Crude contract.

Betting that the price of oil will rise revolves around several factors. At the moment, there is a great deal of unrest in the Middle East, particularly in Libya and Yemen. Trouble in the Middle East means that oil is at risk and thus, the price will (most likely) rise. When things calm down or a peace agreement is reached, it could be a good opportunity to sell oil contracts.

Another important factor is OPEC (Organization of the Petroleum Exporting Countries). You may have heard of it. It basically has a monopoly that controls the price of oil by having member countries limiting exports. When OPEC makes any kind of announcement, it affects the price of oil. Having some kind of keyword alert system via Google Alerts or your trading platform for "OPEC" is a good idea.

There are other factors to consider, of course, but these two are important and you should keep a close eye on what's happening in the Middle East. If you need a hedge, take a look at the ETFs listed next to create a strategy or short airlines, whose stocks usually drop quickly when the price of oil goes higher.

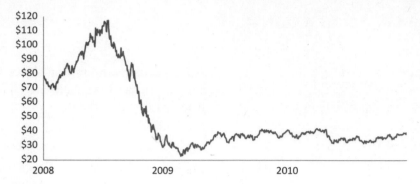

**FIGURE 10.1** Performance of USO Fund ETF since 2008
*Source:* Historical data from Yahoo! Finance

If futures aren't your thing, there are plenty of ETFs that give you exposure to oil. Some are levered, some are inverse, and others just give you easy access to sweet, bubbling crude (and see Figure 10.1):

- United States Oil Fund LP (Ticker: USO)
- United States Brent Oil Fund (Ticker: BNO)
- ProShares Ultra DJ-UBS Crude Oil (Ticker: UCO)
- PowerShares DB Oil Fund (Ticker: DBO)
- iPath S&P GSCI Crude Oil Total Return (Ticker: OIL)
- ProShares Ultra Oil & Gas (Ticker: DIG)
- ProShares UltraShort Oil & Gas (Ticker: DUG)

## Natural Gas

With natural gas, you also have many options. The main futures contract for natural gas is the Henry Hub Natural Gas contract (NG). It's the second-highest volume futures contract in the world based on a physical commodity, according to CME Group.

Be careful trading natural gas. As I previously mentioned, prices are extremely volatile. Reasons for this include prolonged winter weather, resulting in increased demand that exceeds supply, low storage volumes, and difficulties with pipelines used for physical delivery of the gas.

Once in awhile, you'll hear about a gas pipeline exploding somewhere in the United States. This kind of disruption could result in a brief increase in the price of natural gas. See Figure 10.2 for a history of the price of natural gas.

**FIGURE 10.2** Price History of Natural Gas Over the Years
*Source:* U.S. Department of Energy

It is said that Arnold's natural gas trading strategy revolves around trading against the herd when prices have fluctuated away from what he considers fair value. If prices appeared to be topping, you'd consider taking a short position, waiting it out, and hoping for a major drop.

Arnold's bread and butter is still market making in energy markets, so unless you've got a lot of money available at your disposal, it's probably best to speculate by going long or short natural gas based on your own thesis.

If you want to follow a more simplistic strategy, like oil, there are plenty of natural gas ETFs to choose from, including:

- United States Natural Gas Fund, LP (Ticker: UNG)
- First Trust ISE Revere Natural Gas (Ticker: FCG)
- Path Dow Jones-UBS Natural Gas Subindex Total Return (Ticker: GAZ)
- U S 12 Month Natural Gas Fund LP (Ticker: UNL)

Don't forget that you can also go long energy companies directly. Check out names big and small like Exxon-Mobil (XOM), Chevron (CVX), Valero Energy (VLO), Devon Energy (DVN), Flotek Industries (FTK), Western Refining (WNR), Piedmont Natural Gas Company (PNY), Natural Gas Services Group (NGS), Rexx Energy (REXX), Clean Energy Fuels (CLNE), Atlas Energy (ATLS), and the hundreds of other companies involved in the production, delivery, and refining of gas and oil.

## ARNOLD'S TOP TRAITS

It's hard to be as good as Arnold when trading energy. You need to be at the top of your game and know the ins and outs of the energy business. It doesn't hurt to be located in Texas either, where a lot of the industry action occurs. For now, keeps these three important points in mind when you start trading energy:

1. *Pay attention:* Listen to the markets and the news. Energy is a volatile game. You need to be on top of your positions when some kind of news breaks that will affect the price of oil or natural gas, no matter how small. Use big opportunities like the 2010 BP Deepwater Horizon oil spill incident to your advantage. You can short multiple companies even if they haven't done anything wrong just because that's what "the crowd" is doing.

2. *Be different:* As with many of the traders in this book, Arnold has his own way of thinking and trading. He took the other sides of trades when it didn't seem practical. He used Enron's wealth of industry knowledge to his advantage. There are times when it's not good to follow everyone else blindly into a trade. If you feel like oil has peaked, then put your money where your mouth is and short it.

3. *Follow your own rules:* Arnold claims that most of his trading relies on fundamental analysis (as opposed to technical analysis, as performed by Buzzy Schwartz from the previous chapter). Stick to things you understand and use the tips I gave you previously to understand how the markets work in reaction to news. It takes time to make a lot of money.

■  ■  ■

Arnold continues to be incredibly successful, with Centaurus Advisors reportedly managing more than $5 billion in assets as of the beginning of 2011. Despite the firm posting its first-ever yearly loss in 2010 (it was down 4 percent), the firm should continue to go strong if regulation doesn't hamper its strategy. In a post–Dodd-Frank Act world, anything can happen.

Next, we examine four traders who each created vast amounts of wealth for their clients but perhaps shadow others already mentioned in this book.

## CHAPTER 11

# More Great Trades

*Phillip Falcone, David Tepper, Andrew Hall, Greg Lippmann*

W e've come far, and at this point, we have met nearly all of the world's greatest traders: Paulson, Chanos, Bass, Livermore, Jones, Soros, and Templeton. But it could easily be argued that there are many other great traders and investment professionals who deserve credit for reaping equally handsome fortunes. Some of them played similar strategies to the aforementioned greats, while others are unique in their own right.

To list every fund manager or trader who made a fortune in the last 100 years would be a big task, and many of them deployed similar strategies to those already mentioned in this book anyway.

So, this last chapter looks at four traders who we can learn a lot from, for better or worse. They too took healthy profits through their trading strategies and are now positioned to live grandiose lifestyles.

## PHILLIP FALCONE

Phillip Falcone manages Harbinger Capital Partners, one of the biggest hedge funds in America.

Falcone's story is an interesting one. Born in 1962 in the small town of Chisholm, Minnesota, he was an avid hockey player in his youth, a passion that continued with him to Harvard University, where he played varsity hockey and earned a bachelor's degree in Economics. Later on in his life,

Falcone stayed true to his love of the game by purchasing a large stake (rumored to be around 40 percent) in a National Hockey League team, the Minnesota Wild.

Falcone's childhood was not an upper-middle class experience, like, say, John Paulson's was. Falcone was the first person from his high school to attend Harvard. He had eight siblings and his parents worked mediocre jobs—his father was a utility superintendent and his mother, a worker at a T-shirt factory, according to the *Harvard Crimson*. But money would soon not be an issue for Falcone. After graduating from Harvard in 1984, he played briefly for Swedish hockey team Malmo before a career-ending leg injury left him to the world of finance. It's a simple story, really: Guy loves hockey, guy goes to Ivy League school and plays hockey, guy attempts professional hockey career and injures himself, guy ends up on Wall Street.

In 1985, Falcone took his first job in finance with Kidder, Peabody & Co., working on the firm's junk bond—or "high-yield"—desk. He has said that the fit was "natural" for him and that he "wouldn't have been a good investment banker. Patience has never been one of my biggest virtues."[1]

Working on a high-yield desk in the mid-1980s was a time when someone could really earn some serious cash in regard to compensation from bond trading. Michael Milken, for instance, was doing the same thing as Falcone, albeit at a deity-like level of business, at the infamous investment bank Drexel Burnham Lambert. In 1986, Drexel had its best year ever, doing $545.5 million in business, which at the time was the most profitable year for a Wall Street firm *ever*. Milken acquired a $550 million bonus that year. Interestingly, just a few years later, in 1990, Milken and Drexel were charged with multiple crimes by the Securities and Exchange Commission and the firm filed for bankruptcy.

During the late 1990s, Falcone was a senior high-yield bond trader at First Union Capital Markets. He also held various positions with Gleacher-Natwest, an investment bank, and also headed the high-yield trading desk at Barclays Capital.

In 2001, he founded Harbinger Capital Partners. Much of the capital to start the fund was put up by an Alabama-based investment banking house: cofounder Harbert Management Corp. Falcone was named senior managing director of Harbinger Capital Partners and was tasked with generating alpha for the fund's investors.

Falcone made several successful investments for his firm (and some bad choices as well; more on that in a bit), but the two that stand out involve the beginning of the housing crisis in 2006 and the credit crisis, which began in 2007. His first trade was to short one of New York's oldest investment banks, Bear Stearns. Falcone was easily one of the first hedge fund managers to see the writing on the wall at the time and was one of the first to initiate a short position. Bear Stearns's collapse was ultimately attributed to the firm's denial that it was on the wrong side of its bet on the U.S. housing market. Bear kept buying up more and more mortgage-backed securities even as their value dropped. Hank Paulson at the Treasury worked with Bear and J.P. Morgan to arrange a "fire sale" to J.P. Morgan at the price of $10 a share. (Originally, it was to be $2 a share, but Paulson wasn't comfortable with the move.) Falcone's short position must have been quite large in order for Harbinger to add nearly $11 billion to its coffers, putting the firm's assets under management at $26 billion during 2008, according to multiple reports.

And Bear Stearns wasn't the only other bank making awful decisions in regard to housing markets at the time. UK firm HBOS plc (Halifax plc + Bank of Scotland for some context) was also shorted by Falcone. During the fall of 2008, HBOS had liquidity issues and credit problems, and short sellers were putting pressure on the firm's stock. Eventually, famed UK investment house Lloyds TSB purchased HBOS for a mere 232 pence per share. Falcone's short position meant yet another win for the former hockey player.

Another trade that made Harbinger billions of dollars and gave Falcone an $825 million payday in 2009 was shorting the U.S. housing market. Like Kyle Bass and John Paulson, Falcone had the foresight to see that the market's growth up to 2007 was unsustainable and began to short CDOs and asset-backed securities whose underlying assets were horrible mortgages.

It is said that Falcone played commodities markets during 2007 and won big for nine months out of the year. He spent $59 million for a penthouse apartment on New York City's Upper East Side previously owned by *Penthouse* publisher Bob Guccione. Things between Falcone and Harbinger Capital Partners have since changed, though. Harbinger investors are beginning to take redemptions on their investments, worrying about Falcone's biggest investment at the moment: an illiquid, satellite telecom company called LightSquared. Goldman Sachs plans to withdraw up to $120 million in investments in Harbinger, and the Blackstone Group has done the same. Harbinger Capital is now said to have only about $9 billion in assets under management.

Overall, though, it is important to consider what Falcone has achieved. Did he merely get lucky on his bet against the U.S. housing market, or did his experiences on various high-yield bond desks help him hone a successful investment style?

Clearly, Falcone has some tough times ahead as he looks to appease investors and land another big win for Harbinger.

## RECREATING FALCONE'S TRADING STRATEGIES

We've already discussed the various ways to play the housing market a la Paulson and Bass, but let's take a look at some trade suggestions based on Falcone earning his chops on Wall Street trading high-yield junk bonds.

It seems that for every investment strategy on Wall Street, there is an exchange-traded fund to compliment it. Sure enough, if you want to get exposure to junk bonds/high-yield bonds using an ETF, State Street has you covered with its suite of SPDR products. The SPDR Barclays Capital High Yield B ETF (Ticker: JNK) can help you out and you can find a brief description of how the ETF works on its web site.

Figure 11.1 shows the ETF taking a nosedive during the financial crisis, and like many other asset classes, it has been clawing back ever since. As of this writing, it is right around $40. Place your bets on risky bonds, and best of luck to you.

Another trade for Falcone purportedly involved big commodity plays. Since commodities are on a huge tear right now, it may still make sense to hop in the game. Regardless, there are too many strategies to list, so let's examine an ETF that gives us broad exposure to overall commodity markets.

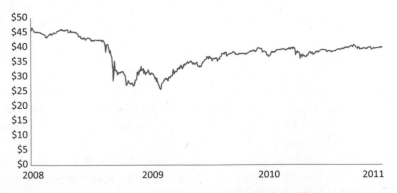

**FIGURE 11.1**   Past Performance of SPDR Lehman High Yield Bond ETF
*Source:* Historical data from Yahoo! Finance

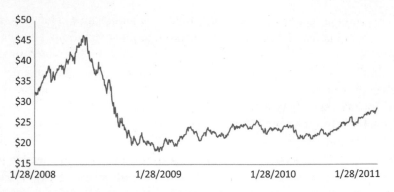

**FIGURE 11.2** Past Performance of PowerShares DB Com Index Tracking Fund ETF
*Source:* Historical data from Yahoo! Finance

Enter the PowerShares DB Com Index Trackng Fund (Ticker: DBC), which is based upon the Deutsche Bank Liquid Commodity Index. It offers wide exposure to a variety of commodities. When the U.S. dollar is weak, this is an ETF that could be a good long position. You could also use it as a portfolio hedge or in a variety of other investment strategies. Figure 11.2 shows how DBC has performed over the past five years. From January 2010 to January 2011, DBC had a return of 21.7 percent—not bad at all.

## DAVID TEPPER

David Tepper, founder of Appaloosa Management, is similar to Phil Falcone in a few ways. His experience comes from work on multiple high-yield trading desks, and Tepper made his investors a lot of money from the financial crisis.

Tepper was born in 1957 and was raised in Pittsburgh, Pennsylvania. It was at the University of Pittsburgh that Tepper earned his BA in economics. While he dabbled with the markets during his youth (the result of watching his father trade), after graduating from college Tepper took a job at Equibank working as a credit and securities analyst. He soon became disappointed with his position and decided it would be best to get his MBA. And so, in 1982, Tepper completed his degree at Carnegie Mellon and took a position at Republic Steel. David's first major position was in 1984 at Keystone Mutual Funds, where he worked on the high-yield desk. In 1985, Goldman Sachs recruited him for its high-yield desk.

As you can see, Falcone and Tepper had similarities. The two were driven, intelligent, and good on the high-yield desk. Goldman recognized Tepper's talents, and he was soon named head of the high-yield desk, a position he held for eight years before forming Appaloosa Management in 1993 in Short Hills, New Jersey. Why leave a prestigious firm such as Goldman Sachs to strike out on your own, you ask? More money.

Jack Walton, a buddy of Tepper's from his days at Goldman, cofounded the hedge fund with him, and Tepper set out to continue his winning streak. Appaloosa is said to have average 30 percent returns year to year since its inception. Taking risks is a big part of investing and trading: If you never take on risk, your reward is bound to be small. Tepper invested heavily in junk bonds and in 2001 generated a 61 percent return for investors.

What I find most interesting about David Tepper is how he benefited from the recovery of the financial crisis rather than from its onset. Tepper's greatest trade is betting that banks would recover in early 2009; he invested in several companies that were bailed out by the Fed, including Bank of America. As the stock market rose throughout 2009, Tepper's bets paid off handsomely, earning Appaloosa around $7 billion for the year.

Tepper's success has enabled him to become a philanthropist, and his biggest contribution to the world thus far has been a $55 million donation to Carnegie Mellon University's business school, where he earned his MBA. It was renamed the David A. Tepper School of Business in his honor.

The latest 13-F statement filed by Appaloosa was on September 30, 2010. It appears that Tepper's largest holdings include shares of online brokerage E-Trade Financial, Bank of America, and health benefits company WellPoint Inc.

Becoming a trader of Tepper's pedigree is quite a challenge. He has an extensive education combined with experience at top financial houses and all the capital he needs. Being able to balance risk and knowing when to initiate positions are just two of the key talents that a top trader like Tepper displays.

## RECREATING TEPPER'S TRADING STRATEGIES

If you want to trade like David Tepper, then you need to be long financials. Whether that is prudent in 2011 remains to be seen.

Consider a financials ETF such as the Financial Select Sector SPDR (Ticker: XLF), which gives you exposure to financial services, insurance, commercial banks, capital markets, real estate investment trusts (REITs), consumer finance, thrifts and mortgage finance, and real estate management and development. If you think America's financial industry is going to recover, then buying XLF would be a good idea. If you think the banks and other financial service providers can't cut it, then shorting XLF is your play.

Figure 11.3 shows the five-year performance of XLF with a –48.3 percent return. Clearly, the industry has a long way to go before it gets back to pre-financial-crisis levels.

You could also enter into a position with a variety of banks. Here are a few of the big ones to consider:

- Bank of America Merrill Lynch (Ticker: BAC)
- Credit Suisse Group AG (Ticker: CS)
- Deutsche Bank (Ticker: DB)
- Goldman Sachs (Ticker: GS)
- Morgan Stanley (Ticker: MS)
- JPMorgan Chase & Co (Ticker: JPM)
- UBS AG (Ticker: UBS)
- Barclays PLC (Ticker: BCS)

Note: Some of the foreign banks trade as American depository receipts (ADRs). They represent ownership in the shares of a non-U.S. company

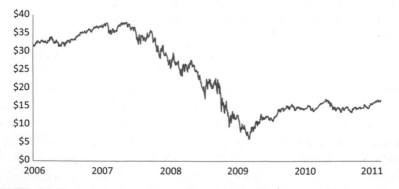

**FIGURE 11.3** Past Performance of Financial Select Sector SPDR ETF
*Source:* Historical data from Yahoo! Finance

that trade in U.S. financial markets and basically allow you to invest in foreign companies. Do your homework when messing with ADRs, as the amount of actual shares an ADR encompasses can vary. In English: One ADR does not equal one share all the time.

## ANDREW HALL

The headlines were out: Andrew J. Hall, a British-born energy trader working in a subset of Citigroup called Phibro, was demanding the bank pay him the $100 million bonus he deserved. The year was 2008.

Phibro was a big profit maker at Citigroup, acting as the firm's proprietary energy trading unit with a focus on oil and gas. When I say a big profit maker, I mean that the group produced $200 million in pretax profits between 1997 and 2009. Here's what the press release from Occidental said after the deal was announced:

> *From 1997 until the second quarter of 2009, Phibro averaged approximately $200 million per year in pre-tax earnings, while over the last five years Phibro's earnings averaged $371 million per year. Phibro has been profitable each fiscal year since 1997, attaining profitability in 80 percent of all quarters.*[2]

Hall had made some extraordinary bets on the energy market back in 2003 when he predicted that long-term and short-term energy prices would become out of sync. Hall's trade was a hell of a bet but, through the use of long-dated options on futures contracts, he bought calls that were most likely *wayyyyy* out of the money. You can do your own research for an introduction to options, but a call gives the buyer the *right* but not the *obligation* to buy an underlying security. They are basic derivatives.

After it was found that, in fact, Hall's trades were the right trades, Citigroup was worried. It was 2009, well into the financial crisis, and the bank owed taxpayers over $45 billion in bailout money. Now it was forced to explain why Hall was due $100 million, his estimated bonus for the year. Why such a large bonus? The controversy surrounding the amount of pay owed to Hall stems from the fact that Hall had apparently negotiated a deal with Citigroup in which he received around 20 percent of profits, according to *Time:*

*Most contracts guaranteed traders around 9% to 11% of their group's profits, before compensation. What's unusual about Hall is that he reportedly receives as much as 20% of his unit's profits, which sets him up for much bigger paydays than the rest of the Street.*[3]

So where is Hall today? Did he get his big payday after all was said and done? After all, Citi (and most likely Tim Geithner at the Treasury) fought to curtail the dollar amount Hall was owed. In the end, Phibro was eventually sold to Occidental Petroleum for $250 million with a fat guarantee that ensured Hall was paid adequately. The exact terms of the deal are not known to the public, but here's what the aforementioned press release about the Citi-Phibro deal said about Mr. Andrew Hall:

*Phibro's management team, headed by Andrew Hall, and its employees will remain with the company after closing. The senior management team has agreed to make a significant investment in Phibro and receive returns dependent upon the company's future performance. Additionally, significant portions of current and future bonuses will be deferred and retained by Phibro and paid out in future years. These future payouts will be adjusted to reflect Phibro's results during that period.*[4]

Hall now owns an amazing, 1,000-year-old castle in Germany called SchlosseDerneberg. It houses a large part of his massive art collection and is closed to the public. You need to schedule a private appointment for a tour.

As far as art goes, Hall frustrated and angered his neighbors in Southport, Connecticut, by displaying an 82-foot-long concrete sculpture by Anselm Kiefer. After a four-year battle, he was ordered to remove the sculpture. I am positive it is the least of Andrew Hall's worries.

## RECREATING HALL'S TRADING STRATEGIES

Hall is an energy man. He focused primarily on oil and gas while at Citigroup, so we shall talk about that here. First, look at the ProShares Ultra DJ-UBS Crude Oil (Ticker: UCO). This bad boy corresponds to twice the daily performance of the Dow Jones—UBS Crude Oil Sub-Index. In other

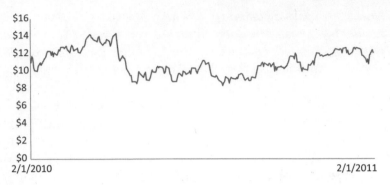

**FIGURE 11.4**  Past Performance of ProShares Ultra DJ-UBS Crude Oil ETF
*Source:* Historical data from Yahoo! Finance

words, it's a 200 percent levered ETF. If the UBS index goes up, you make 2X the performance, and the same goes for losses.

Using UCO, you can make big bets on the oil markets while having ample liquidity and adequate leverage. There are also other oil-related ETFs, such as OIH, USO, DIG, DUG, and UCO's short-selling cousin, SCO.

Figure 11.4 shows the one year performance of UCO. Clearly, it is best for short-term plays based upon global events or factors related to the price of oil. For instance, if you wanted to play an OPEC announcement, UCO or SCO would be a fine choice as an instrument for doing so.

Also, there is the Energy Select Sector SPDR (Ticker: XLE), which tracks the energy sector of the S&P 500. Energy companies in the index include crude producers, natural gas producers, and companies that provide drilling and other energy-related services. Figure 11.5 shows the one-year

**FIGURE 11.5**  Past Performance of Energy Select Sector SPDR ETF
*Source:* Historical data from Yahoo! Finance

performance of XLE. From September 2010 to January 1, 2011, XLE shot higher thanks to a rally in equities and a rise in the price of both oil and natural gas.

## GREG LIPPMANN

Greg Lippmann is thought of by some to be somewhat of a wiseass, but he's one hell of a trader. If you'll recall, Lippmann was the guy in Michael Lewis's latest tale of finance, *The Big Short*, that reportedly passed around shirts at Deutsche Bank that read, "I'm Short Your House." He has since moved on to bigger, better, and more mature things, but Lippmann is a legend in his own right. Like other people in this book (Kyle Bass, John Paulson), Lippmann was one of the first guys on the Street to see the mortgage mess coming long before it was on anyone else's mind.

Greg was running the subprime mortgage desk at Deutsche Bank, back in the fall of 2005, when it struck him that the U.S. housing market was unsustainable. He called up Michael Burry, principal of Scion Capital. Burry was essentially unknown until Lewis came out with *The Big Short* and the *New York Times* and others did profiles on his short-housing call. According to reports, Lippmann was shorting the housing market to the tune of $1 billion, a risk so large it's hard to fathom how management at Deutsche Bank even let him get away with the trade.

Loud and outspoken, Lippmann soon sauntered over to a hedge fund by the name of FrontPoint partners, run by Steve Eisman—yet another great trader who surely deserves a chapter in a book. Lippmann pitched Eisman and his team on the idea of shorting the housing market. Like Bass, Lippmann saw that housing prices were ripping higher and higher year over year and that this growth couldn't last forever. Again, we go back to the theme of borrowers not understanding the basic concepts of credit and how an adjustable-rate mortgage works. This presents at least one problem in that the American homeowner needs to be a better educated consumer. No matter. Greg Lippmann saw dollar signs and went after them as quickly as he could. In other words, homeowners were probably going to be unable to pay their mortgages sooner rather than later. If you want to know why Lippmann was (reportedly) giving out shirts that said "I'm Short Your House," Figure 11.6 shows you exactly what Lippmann had in mind.

The funny thing is that nearly every investment bank on the Street, including Deutsche Bank, was busy packaging these awful mortgages into

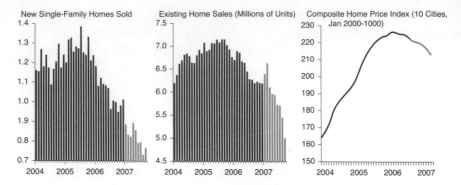

**FIGURE 11.6** The U.S. Housing Market Takes A Turn For The Worse in 2007
*Source:* FDIC.gov

bonds, getting them rated AAA by the ratings agencies and selling them to one another. In 2007, Deutsche Bank bought a mortgage lender called MortgageIT, which specialized in creating so-called Alt-A mortgages (a grade higher than junk status). It ended up costing the bank over $20 billion in balance sheet writedowns. One can't help imagine Greg Lippmann laughing candidly at lunch at how stupidly the banks were acting.

Lippmann spent the next few months buying credit default swaps on different CDOs and mortgage-backed securities. It was like taking out an insurance policy on some broke guy with a fat mortgage and paying a really small premium per year. At one point, AIG was reportedly selling credit default swaps on mortgage bonds for around 15 basis points. On the road, Lippman was pitching everyone he thought might be interested, including Michael Burry at Scion Capital, Phil Falcone at Harbinger Capital, and Eisman at FrontPoint. The plan worked and Lippmann was essentially set. Like clockwork, the housing industry took a turn for the worse, homeowner defaults rocketed skyward, and Deutsche Bank ended up having to offer Greg Lippmann a $50 million bonus.

Ultimately, Lippmann made over $2 billion for Deutsche Bank during the housing crisis, according to Bloomberg.[5] Today, Lippmann runs a hedge fund called LibreMax, which has between $325 million and $1 billion under management, depending on who you're talking to. He started it with another fellow from Deutsche Bank: Fred Brettschneider. And if that weren't enough, Lippmann ended up poaching essentially his entire former desk at Deutsche. He even got his hands on Eugene Xu, a famous quantitative analyst who helped Lippmann do his trades on Deutsche's asset-backed securities desk.

Dedication runs deep on Wall Street (to an extent, of course), and LibreMax shows that. Lippmann is now positioned to make money off the recovery of the U.S. housing market after shorting the living daylights out of it. He expects the housing market to go down another 10 percent but claims it won't pose the same kind of problem to the financial system as it did a few years ago.

> *If housing prices go down 10 percent, the mortgage market is going to do fine because that's what is priced in," Lippmann said in an interview with Bloomberg. "Broader markets aren't pricing in housing down another 10 percent.*[6]

Some might resent the trades that Lippmann pulled off. In an interview with the *New York Observer*, a reporter asked him if he appeared to come off as "dickish." Lippmann's response?

> *If you're a die-hard Yankee fan, and you meet someone who's a die-hard Red Sox fan, there's an initial "He's a dick,' right? Because he likes the Red Sox and I like the Yankees." So the people that were rabidly bullish about this, that had invested their own careers on the opposite of me, it's natural they'd be like, "Well, that guy's a dick, because he disagrees with me. He's not a dick for any credible reason. He's a dick because I don't like his opinion."*[7]

At this point, the one thing that remains in question about Greg Lippmann is the fate of his infamous sushi spreadsheet. On the Internet, the most recent copy available is from late 2004 and features more than 100 rankings of sushi joints throughout New York City ranked by neighborhood, taste, and price. His top pick? Jewel Bako in the East Village.

## RECREATING LIPPMANN'S TRADING STRATEGIES

Unless you're dealing with some serious cash, chances are you'll be unable to call up your broker and short mortgage-backed securities. Luckily,

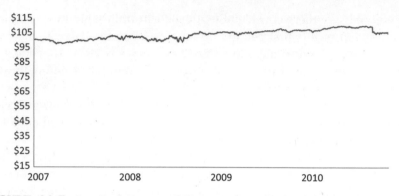

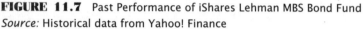

**FIGURE 11.7**   Past Performance of iShares Lehman MBS Bond Fund
*Source:* Historical data from Yahoo! Finance

as with many other strategies in this book, we have an ETF that can help us gain exposure to mortgage-backed securities. We'll be using the iShares Lehman MBS Bond Fund (Ticker: MBB), which is offered by BlackRock iShares. You can read more about the fund online by doing your own research. So if you think home prices are going up and people are rushing to their banks for mortgages, then you would want to go long MBB. Conversely, if you had the mind-set of Lippmann, you would short MBB. Figure 11.7 shows the five-year performance of MBB. The recovery it's had since mid-2008 is impressive considering the economic conditions. But toward the end of 2010, MBB fell from $110 to $105 a share rather quickly, and that downward trend looks to have continued into January and February 2011. Since then, it has bounced back somewhat but has yet to reach the $110 level again.

## IN SUMMARY

After reading the stories in this book, you can clearly see that traders today face more challenges than ever. The markets have evolved considerable since Livermore's heyday and even the crash of 1987.

The Dodd-Frank Act and specifically the Volcker rule put in place in 2010 will have the biggest impact on markets. These regulations are still nebulous as the Securities and Exchange Commission and Commodity Futures Trading Commission debate the proper way to define the rules set forth by Dodd-Frank.

Not only are there considerable regulatory hurdles, but there is also a new breed of twenty-first century trader who looks to challenge the markets with sophisticated algorithms and low-latency trading. This is not to say that so-called high-frequency trading is a bad thing. It is merely an evolution of the electronic trader.

Still, no matter the outcome, plenty of traders out there are destined to become greats. Should Jack Schwager still be around, he will no doubt include their names in his new iterations of *Market Wizards*.

Names that stick out include hedge fund manager David Rucker. His fund, Golden Archer Investments, will use high-frequency trading to capture more profits using proprietary arbitrage strategies. Golden Archer's chief technological officer William Yeack will help lead this charge. I expect both men to do great things and make a lot of money.

Evan McDaniel is another name that comes to mind. Currently helping subscribers of Drakon Capital's stockMONSTER service make money, Evan is the epitome of a professional day trader. His knowledge of the options and futures markets will lead him to start a fund, and his P&L sheet tells the tale of a successful young man.

Wesley Harr, also at Drakon Capital, will similarly parlay his money into great sums with his in-depth knowledge of a multitude of stocks and options.

In the end, it doesn't matter how much capital you start with or what strategy you employ. What matters is sticking to your trading thesis and adjusting it to do only two things: create profits and minimize losses.

# Notes

## CHAPTER 2

1. http://en.wikipedia.org/wiki/Enron

## CHAPTER 3

1. www.turtletrader.com/paul-tudor-jones-interview.html

## CHAPTER 5

1. Kindleberger, Charles P., and Aliber, Robert. (2005). *Manias, Panics, and Crashes: A History of Financial Crises* (5th ed.). Hoboken, NJ: John Wiley & Sons.
2. www.unrulydog.com/JLPlacid.html
3. Smitten, Richard. (2001). *Jesse Livermore: The World's Greatest Stock Trader.* New York: John Wiley & Sons, p. 281.
4. www.unrulydog.com/JLPlacid.html

## CHAPTER 6

1. www.pionline.com/article/20070709/FACETOFACE/70705017
2. www.portfolio.com/executives/features/2009/01/07/John-Paulson-Profits-in-Downturn/
3. www.cnbc.com/id/38789781/Hedge_Fund_Heavyweight_Paulson_Makes_New_Housing_Bet

## CHAPTER 8

1. www.nytimes.com/2009/02/01/business/01gret.html
2. www.snl.com/IRWebLinkX/file.aspx?IID=4092627&FID=9298100

3. 3.www.nytimes.com/2010/03/12/business/12lehman.html?_r=1&pagewanted=1&hp&adxnnlx=1268399443-LeJIn2Z9sQ%20lvnGaoI0fqw

4. nymag.com/news/businessfinance/47844/

## CHAPTER 9

1. Schwartz, Martin. (1999). *Pitbull: Lessons from Wall Street's Champion Day Trader*. Haper Paperbacks.

2. http://marketstockwatch.blogspot.com/2006/07/listen-to-martin-buzzy-schwartz.html

## CHAPTER 10

1. www.nytimes.com/2002/07/09/business/corporate-conduct-the-trader-enron-trader-had-a-year-to-boast-of-even-if.html?pagewanted=2&src=pm

2. http://replay.waybackmachine.org/20080616105737/http://www.nymex.com/cur_article_011805.aspx

3. www.cftc.gov/ucm/groups/public/@newsroom/documents/file/hearing080509_arnold.pdf

4. www.gata.org/node/4753

## CHAPTER 11

1. www.thecrimson.com/article/2009/6/2/class-of-1984-philip-a-falcone/

2. www.oxy.com/News_Room/Pages/News_Release.aspx?releaseid=175149

3. www.time.com/time/business/article/0,8599,1930732,00.html#ixzz17OwhIxHC

4. www.oxy.com/News_Room/Pages/News_Release.aspx?releaseid=175149

5. www.bloomberg.com/news/2010-12-02/u-s-home-prices-to-drop-additional-10-says-subprime-investor-lippmann.html

6. www.bloomberg.com/news/2010-12-02/u-s-home-prices-to-drop-additional-10-says-subprime-investor-lippmann.html

7. www.observer.com/2010/wall-street/mr-bubble-bounces-back

# Glossary

**Arbitrage**    The simultaneous purchase and sale of an asset in order to profit from a difference in the price. It is a trade that profits by exploiting price differences of identical or similar financial instruments, on different markets, or in different forms. Arbitrage exists as a result of market inefficiencies; it provides a mechanism to ensure that prices do not deviate substantially from fair value for long periods.

**Bonds**    A fancy word for debt. Bonds are debt investments in which an investor lends money to an entity that borrows the funds for a defined period of time at a fixed interest rate.

**Collateralized Debt Obligation (CDO)**    An investment-grade security backed by a pool of bonds, loans, and other assets. CDOs do not specialize in one type of debt but are often nonmortgage loans or bonds.

**Credit Default Swap (CDS)**    A swap designed to transfer the credit exposure of fixed income products between parties.

**Dark Pools of Liquidity**    The trading volume created by institutional orders that are unavailable to the public. The bulk of dark pool liquidity is represented by block trades facilitated away from the central exchanges.

**Derivatives**    A security whose price is dependent upon or derived from one or more underlying assets. A contract between parties. Derivatives are a zero sum game (i.e. if one side loses, the other side wins). There are four major kinds of derivatives: options, futures, forwards, and swaps.

**Equities**    Another term for stocks. An instrument that signifies an ownership position, or equity, in a corporation, and represents a claim on its proportionate share in the corporation's assets and profits.

**Exchange**    A marketplace in which securities, commodities, derivatives, and other financial instruments are traded.

**Federal Funds Rate**    The interest rate at which a depository institution lends immediately available funds (balances at the Federal Reserve) to another depository institution overnight.

**Forward**    A cash market transaction in which delivery of the commodity is deferred until after the contract has been made. Although the delivery is made in the future, the price is determined on the initial trade date. Unlike futures, forwards are not traded on an exchange.

**Futures**   A financial contract obligating the buyer to purchase an asset (or the seller to sell an asset), such as a physical commodity or a financial instrument, at a predetermined future date and price.

**Hedge Fund**   In the most basic terms, a hedge fund is an investment partnership that accepts large sums of money that invests in a number of assets using a number of strategies.

**LIBOR**   London Interbank Offered Rate. An interest rate at which banks can borrow funds, in marketable size, from other banks in the London interbank market.

**Mortgage-Backed Security (MBS)**   A type of asset-backed security that is secured by a mortgage or collection of mortgages and rated by a ratings agency like S&P or Moody's.

**Mutual Fund**   An investment vehicle that is made up of a pool of funds collected from many investors for the purpose of investing in securities such as stocks, bonds, money market instruments, and similar assets.

**Options**   A contract that that offers the buyer the right, but not the obligation, to buy (call) or sell (put) a security or other financial asset at an agreed-upon price (the strike price) during a certain period of time or on a specific date (exercise date).

**Prime Rate**   The interest rate that commercial banks charge their most creditworthy customers.

**Proprietary Trading**   Simply put: using principal or "house money" to speculate in the market.

**Securitization**   Securitization is the process of taking an illiquid asset, or group of assets, and through financial engineering transforming them into a security.

**Speculator**   A trader with higher-than-average risk in return for a higher-than-average return.

**Swap**   The exchange of one security for another to change the maturity (bonds), quality of issues (stocks or bonds), or investment objectives.

**Synthetic Collateralized Debt Obligation**   A form of collateralized debt obligation (CDO) that invests in credit default swaps (CDSs) or other noncash assets to gain exposure to a portfolio of fixed income assets.

# References

## CHAPTER 1

Bass, Kyle. Personal Interview. March 10, 2010.

Investopedia. "Mortgaged-Backed Security." Last accessed April 2010. www.investopedia.com/terms/m/mbs.asp.

Durbin, Michael. *All About Derivatives*. New York: McGraw-Hill, 2005.

Kreisler, Jeff. *Get Rich Cheating: The Crooked Path to Easy Street*. New York: Harper Paperbacks, 2009.

Paulson, Henry. *On the Brink: Inside the Race to Stop the Collapse of the Global Financial System*. Boston, Massachusetts: Business Plus, 2010.

Federal Reserve. "Board of Governors of the Federal Reserve System." Last accessed June 2010. www.federalreserve.gov.

Yahoo! Finance. "Symbol Lookup from Yahoo! Finance." Last accessed October 2010. finance.yahoo.com/lookup?s=Historical+Prices.

## CHAPTER 2

Chanos, James. Personal Interview. April 2010.

McClean, Bethany, and Elkind, Peter. *The Smartest Guys in the Room: The Amazing Rise and Scandalous Fall of Enron*. New York, New York: Portfolio Trade, 2004.

Wikipedia. "Products." Last accessed May 2010. en.wikipedia.org/wiki/Enron.

Yahoo! Finance. "Symbol Lookup from Yahoo! Finance." Last accessed June 2010. finance.yahoo.com/lookup?s=Historical+Prices.

## CHAPTER 3

Burton, Katherine. "Adapt or Die." *Hedge Funds Review*. July 2004: 19–20. www.hedgefundsreview.com/global/hedgefundsreview/fund_profiles/T/04_Jul_-_Tudor_Inv_Corp.pdf.

Elliot, R. N. "The Basis of the Wave Principle." 1940.

Jones, Paul Tudor. "Interview with Paul Tudor Jones II." Joel Ramin. January 13, 2000. www.absolutereturn-alpha.com/Article/1964189/Paul-Tudor-Jones-II.html.

Jones, Paul Tudor. "Paul Tudor Jones II." Stephen Taub. June 30, 2008. www.absolutereturn-alpha.com/Article/1964189/Paul-Tudor-Jones-II.html.

Jones, Paul Tudor. "Tudor Returns to Its Roots." Stephen Taub. August 31, 2010. www.absolutereturn-alpha.com/Article/2657707/Tudor-returns-to-its-roots.html.

"Introduction to Global Macro Hedge Funds." Nicholas, Joseph G. *Inside the House of Money*. n.d. http://media.wiley.com/product_data/excerpt/73/04717944/0471794473.pdf.

Schwager, J. D. "Market Wizards: Interviews with Top Traders." 1992. www.absolutereturn-alpha.com/Article/2657707/Tudor-returns-to-its-roots.html.

Jones, P.T. (2009) "Perfect Failure." Commencement speech to the Buckley School. www.scribd.com/doc/16588637/Paul-Tudor-Jones-Failure-Speech-June-2009.

Vimeo. "Trader: 1987—PTJ." Last accessed December 2010. http://vimeo.com/9881971.

## CHAPTER 4

Herrmann, Robert. "Sir John Templeton." *Business Times*. (June, 1998).

"Franklin to Acquire Templeton Mutual fund," *Business Times*, p. 8 (August 3, 1992).

Franklin Templeton Investments. "History of Franklin Resources Inc." Last accessed December 2010. www.franklinresources.com/corp/pages/generic_content/about_us/history.jsf.

The John Templeton Foundation. "The John Templeton Foundation." Last accessed November 2010. www.templeton.org.

## CHAPTER 5

Lefevre, Edwin. *Reminiscences of a Stock Operator, Annotated Edition*. Hoboken, New Jersey: John Wiley & Sons, 2009.

Investopedia. "Bucket Shop Definition." Last accessed October 2010. www.investopedia.com/terms/b/bucketshop.asp.

The Federal Reserve Bank of Boston. "Panic of 1907." Last accessed October 2010. www.bos.frb.org/about/pubs/panicof1.pdf.

Home of the Unruly Dog. "Extracts from The Lake Placid News." Last accessed November, 2010. www.unrulydog.com/JLPlacid.html.

Brown, Joshua. Personal Interview. November 2010.

## CHAPTER 6

Hedge Fund News. "John Paulson—Paulson & Co." Last accessed November 2010. www.hedgefundnews.com/news_n_info/article_detail.php?id=292.

Federal Reserve Board. "What You Should Know about a Home Equity Line of Credit." Last accessed November 2010. www.federalreserve.gov/pubs/equity/equity_english.htm.

Lewis, Michael. *The Big Short: Inside the Doomsday Machine.* New York, New York: W. W. Norton & Company, 2010.

Yahoo! Finance. "Paulson Point Man on CDO Deal Emerges as Key Figure." Last accessed October 2010. finance.yahoo.com/retirement/article/109342/paulson-point-man-on-cdo-deal-emerges-as-key-figure?mod=retire&sec=topStories&pos=2&asset=&ccode=.

Zuckerman, Gregory. *The Greatest Trade Ever: The Behind-the-Scenes Story of How John Paulson Defied Wall Street and Made Financial History.* New York, New York: Crown Business, 2010.

## CHAPTER 7

George Soros. "George Soros." Last accessed November 2010. www.georgesoros.com

Slater, Robert. *Soros: The Life, Time and Trading Secrets of the World's Greatest Investor.* Columbus, Ohio: McGraw-Hill, 1997.

Path Lights Press. "Who Is George Soros?" Last accessed December 2010. www.pathlightspress.com/soros.html.

## CHAPTER 8

foolingsomepeople.com/main/.

www.nytimes.com/2009/01/04/opinion/04lewiseinhorn.html.

www.fool.com/investing/dividends-income/2007/01/17/how-allied-capital-won-the-war.aspx.

www.forbes.com/2008/05/16/einhorn-allied-capital-oped-books-cx_hc_0516book review.html

nymag.com/news/businessfinance/47844/.

www.marketrap.com/article/view_article/91218/ares-capital-allied-capital-and-david-einhorn-the-predator-in-a-cute-t-shirt.

## CHAPTER 9

Schwartz, Martin. *Pit Bull: Lessons from Wall Street's Champion Day Trader*. New York, New York: Harper Paperbacks, 1999.

Schwager, Jack D. *Market Wizards: Interviews with Top Traders*. New York, New York: Harper Paperbacks, 1992.

## CHAPTER 10

money.cnn.com/2009/11/23/news/companies/centaurus_john_arnold.fortune/.

www.marketwatch.com/story/amaranth-collapse-leaves-john-arnold-atop-energy-hedge-fund-heap.

www.cftc.gov/ucm/groups/public/@newsroom/documents/file/hearing080509_arnold.pdf.

www.gata.org/node/4753.

www.edhec-risk.com/site_edhecrisk/public/features/RISKArticle.2006-10-02.0711.

## CHAPTER 11

Traders Log. "Top Hedge Fund Managers—Phil Falcone Harbinger Capital Partners—Traders Log." Last accessed November 2010. www.traderslog.com/falcone/

Stewart, James B. *Den of Thieves*. New York, New York: Touchstone Books, 1992.

Lewis, Michael. *The Big Short: Inside the Doomsday Machine*. New York, New York: W. W. Norton & Company, 2010.

*New York Observer*. "Mr. Bubble Bounces Back." Last accessed October 2010. www.observer.com/2010/wall-street/mr-bubble-bounces-back.

*Time.* "Wall Street: How Andrew Hall Earned His Citigroup Pay." Last accessed December 2010. www.time.com/time/business/article/0,8599,1930732,00.html

*The Telegraph.* "Citi Trader Andrew Hall Fights for $100 Million Bonus." Last accessed November 2010. www.telegraph.co.uk/finance/newsbysector/banksandfinance/5908047/Citi-trader-Andrew-Hall-fights-for-100m-bonus.html.

Carnegie Mellon Tepper School of Business. "About David Tepper." Last accessed November 2010. web.tepper.cmu.edu/tepper/about.aspx.

*International Business Times.* "Who Is David Tepper?" Last accessed January 2011. www.ibtimes.com/articles/103669/20110121/who-is-david-tepper-the-story-of-a-billionaire-hedge-fund-manager.htm#.

# Helpful Web Sites

Whether you're an amateur trader or a market veteran, the following web sites are a treasure trove of knowledge, education, and entertainment related to trading and the world of finance.

**10Q Detective (http://10qdetective.blogspot.com/)**
This blog covers 8-K and 10-Q filings with the SEC—particularly interesting for those looking to spot the next Enron.

**AVC (www.avc.com)**
Those of you interested in the business of venture capital can follow Union Square Ventures' Fred Wilson through his blog.

**Albourne Village (village.albourne.com)**
Reserved for financial professionals, this private community offers up a plethora of information and networks that will help nearly anyone with their job.

**Barron's (www.barrons.com)**
Still one of the traditional investment publications and cousin to the Wall Street Journal. Good for reading over the weekend for new trading ideas.

**Bespoke Investment Group (www.bespokeinvest.com)**
Bespoke offers up posts on a variety of financial topics and has great sets of data that are both informative and useful.

**Bloomberg (www.bloomberg.com)**
The undisputed king of financial markets, Bloomberg offers broad access to a large array of data plus up-to-the-minute news and informative editorial pieces.

**Chicago Board Options Exchange (www.cboe.com)**
Chicago's biggest options exchange offers up everything you need to know on how options work and how to trade them at CBOE.

**CME Group (www.cmegroup.com)**
If you're going to trade futures, then you're going to probably deal with CME Group. CME is the world's leading derivatives marketplace and has enough contracts to make your head spin.

**Daily FX (www.dailyfx.com)**

If you're into forex trading, then Daily FX is a decent place, with its wide array of news and analysis.

**Dealbook (http://dealbook.nytimes.com)**

Edited by *Too Big to Fail* author Andrew Ross Sorkin, Dealbook from the *New York Times* focuses on the M&A community and the buy-side. Always a good read.

**Dealbreaker (www.dealbreaker.com)**

Editor Bess Levin takes on Wall Street's biggest firms with a witty sense of humor. It's great comic relief when your day becomes too serious.

**Finviz (www.finviz.com)**

Finviz has one of the best stock screeners, as well as a trove of information on futures and forex markets. There's also a set of interactive heat maps.

**FINalternatives (www.finalternatives.com)**

Anyone looking for daily news on hedge funds that matter should check out FINalternatives.

**Financial Times (www.ft.com)**

If you think the *Wall Street Journal* is too "American" for your liking, then check out its UK cousin, *Financial Times*. I tend to like the print version more than the online content.

**Grant's Interest Rate Observer (www.grantspub.com)**

A decent collection of online news in e-magazine format. Decent cartoons, too.

**Hamzei Analytics (www.hamzeianalytics.com)**

Fari Hamzei offers webinars and data to help you be the best trader. His proprietary algorithms are something else.

**Hedge Accordingly (www.hedgeaccording.ly)**

Run by day trader Evan McDaniel, this web site provides great market commentary, charts, and a dash of humor.

**HedgeFundNet (www.hedgefund.net)**

A great source for both data and news on the hedge fund industry, good for both those working within the hedge fund industry and those merely observing it.

**High Water women (www.highwaterwomen.org)**

Though many women haven't been mentioned in this book, professionals working in finance should check out this web site and organization, which focuses on teaching financial literacy and helping out charities.

**iBankCoin (www.ibankcoin.com)**

iBankCoin contains in-house blogger commentary that's absurdly funny. The site is led by its epic founder, "The Fly."

**Link to Wall Street (www.linktowallstreet.com)**

Those looking for a job on Wall Street can find a collection of recruiters and job offers on this web site. It is aimed at the seasoned professional rather than the amateur trader.

**Market Folly (www.marketfolly.com)**

Market Folly tracks the portfolios of 40-plus prominent hedge funds on a daily basis and offers up commentary on the industry's biggest players.

**Markets Media (www.marketsmediaonline.com)**

The web site for the company I (as of this writing) work for. Online content complements the magazine and live conferences. A subscription is required.

**Planet Money (www.npr.org/money)**

National Public Radio's Planet Money has a fantastic podcast that airs a few times a week. The team covers everything from macroeconomic events to the intricacies of mortgage-backed securities.

**Seeking Alpha (www.seekingalpha.com)**

Financial professionals from all over the globe come here to share their opinions on the markets.

**StockTwits (www.stocktwits.com)**

StockTwits harnesses the power of Twitter and crowdsourcing to bring financial data and market sentiment from Twitter to your computer screen.

**Reuters (www.reuters.com)**

Reuters is similar to Bloomberg, offering breaking news and in-depth coverage of everything related to finance.

**SecondMarket (www.secondmarket.com)**

Want to invest in private companies like Facebook and Groupon? This is one of the few ways you can do it.

**Techmeme (www.techmeme.com)**

Any serious tech investor or enthusiast can keep up to date with the latest news and market stories that are relevant on Techmeme. It's one of my favorite news aggregators.

**The Altucher Confidential (http://www.jamesaltucher.com/)**

James Altucher's personal web site is full of ludicrous tales of 1990s greed and poor investment decisions. If you want a break from work, get a dose of reality at his site The Altucher Confidential.

**The Big Picture (www.ritholtz.com)**

Barry Ritholtz's blog features witty, crafty, and sound advice from one of the Street's coolest money managers.

***The Economist* (www.economist.com)**

You've seen the magazine, but the web site for *The Economist* is full of short, inspiring stories that can give you new ideas for investing.

**The Reformed Broker (www.reformedbroker.com)**

My buddy Joshua Brown runs this tongue-in-cheek web site covering everything in the world in finance. Check it out in the morning and during your lunch break.

**The Wall Street Journal (www.wsj.com)**

I shouldn't need to say anything more about this. If you're not reading the Journal on a daily basis, you should start now.

**Thomson StreetSight (www.streetsight.net)**

Thomson's StreetSight might cost you a few bucks, but it offers up nearly everyone's e-mail and phone number within the industry—Paul Tudor Jones included.

**Traders Magazine (www.tradersmagazine.com)**

An older magazine in the investment community, but full of news on smaller firms and what the little guys are up to.

**U.S. Bureau of Labor Statistics (www.bls.gov)**

The BLS is jam-packed with enough economic figures, data, and charts to make your head spin. It's a great source for getting historical economic data.

**Zerohedge (www.zerohedge.com)**

Zerohedge isn't for everyone. It's big with the bear and doom-and-gloom crowd, but always has a really good read on it.

# Index